The Dilemmas of African Independence

THE WALKER SUMMIT LIBRARY No. 3

The Dilemmas of African Independence

L. Gray Cowan
Columbia University

WALKER AND COMPANY • NEW YORK

$C 67$

Squires

iv

FOREWORD

In this book Professor Cowan singles out the major questions confronting the new African states today. He analyzes them with clarity and penetration and points up the numerous dilemmas in which the new countries find themselves. He presents a picture of the hopes and aspirations of the leadership and the peoples combined with profound difficulties and serious unresolved problems.

This new Africa of more than thirty independent states came into being with startling suddenness. The breakup of empire and the creation of independent states affecting all of South Asia, nearly all of Africa, and other parts of the world has been one of the startling developments of our generation. Although the movement toward independence, especially relating to the Indian Sub-Continent, developed momentum between the two world wars, the sweeping developments in this field belong to the period since 1945. India, Pakistan, Ceylon and Burma obtained their independence at the close of the war, and French and Dutch possessions in Asia obtained nationhood soon thereafter.

In Africa the Italian colonies were transformed to nationhood under the aegis of the United Nations, and Tunisia and Morocco, former French possessions, became independent.

These major beginnings in the decline of empire were followed in the late fifties by the creation of many new nations south of the Sahara. The final chapter in the transformation of territory to statehood is about to be written.

"The winds of change" so powerfully reflected in the territories of Africa were also given vocal expression in the halls of the United Nations. Already in 1945 the political, economic, social and educational rights of these people were clearly set forth by the authors of the United Nations Charter in chapters 11, 12 and 13 of their document, a virtual Magna Carta of non-self-governing people, and self-determination and independence were established as their goals.

Petitioners from African communities appeared before appropriate United Nations organs in increasing numbers and frequency, and as nations became independent and assumed membership in the United Nations the active weight of the United Nations was thrown more and more toward an acceleration of the independence movement.

An important landmark in the acceleration of independence came through the adoption by the 15th session of the General Assembly in 1960-61 of the anti-colonial resolution, which contained the important clause that the political readiness and economic liability of a territory should not be taken into account in the determination of the schedule of independence. Those opposing the resolution thought a more moderate pace would be desirable. Those favoring the resolution emphasized the basic rights of peoples to be independent as well as the conviction that delays would not accelerate the readiness of a people for independence. The Committee of 17 (now 24) set up the following year, pursuant to this Resolution, continues today to be the active and vital organ in the United Nations concerned with the final liquidation of colonial territories.

Independence for most former colonial peoples is today a fact. There are some similarities in the problems with which they have to cope as well as some significant variations. Many of them are still lacking an adequate corps of trained administrators. Central government in those cases is consequently weak and lacks the nationwide efficiency and even-handed contribution to the maintenance of law and order which they will want ultimately to achieve. A closely related problem is the espousal of national unity which is often sought through efforts to secure popular acceptance of ideological patterns rather than through effective administration. Nationalism, which is the necessary weapon to achieve unity, often runs into conflict with established cultural traditions.

Professor Cowan also deals with the issues of modernization and westernization as opposed to the strong currents toward Africanization of these new nations. The understandable desire to break with the past, and in some cases to overcompensate in that break, may inflict new economic and political wounds upon the lives of these states. Yet these people, whether at this stage or in other stages of their national evolution, will learn for themselves and determine the degree to which the assistance proffered by others as well as the governmental, legal and other practices of others may be built into the infra-structure of their national life.

This is a period of immense historical significance for all the new nations and a time when their collective labors, insight and wisdom are needed in full measure if unity, stability, growth and peace are to be their lot.

ANDREW W. CORDIER
Dean, Faculty of International Affairs,
Columbia University

PREFACE

In a report on the program and doctrine of the Parti de la Fédération Africaine, delivered in 1959, Léopold Senghor, the President of Senegal, concluded that "the Nation is the first reality of the twentieth century." The leaders of African nationalism have been striving to bring about the reality of the Nation in the African continent over the past two decades in their struggle to create independent states out of colonial territories. But the new political units which have resulted from their efforts are as yet by no means always Nations; rather, they represent the shells of territorial independence in which the kernel of national identity has been planted by the independence movements. It now becomes the task of the new governments to provide the soil in which the seed can grow.

The consolidation of national independence in Africa will be much more difficult than was its formal acquisition. The problems of devising a satisfactory post-independence political framework were given scant attention during the years of mobilization of popular support against colonial rule. Since coming into power, the leaders have been absorbed in the immediate tasks of governing and in the urgent drive for economic progress.

Regardless of their present preoccupations, however, they are rapidly being faced with the need to make fundamental choices in both internal and external policies, choices which will affect the future of their countries for many years to come. The structure and philosophy of government they lay down now and the direction which they give to future development will ultimately decide whether the fruits of independence ripen into full sweetness or wither into bitter disillusionment.

The conflict between the drive for technical advance which will mean the material enrichment of the lives of the mass of the African people, and the need to preserve those elements of the African cultural heritage that are threatened by the modernizing process, is now, after a few years of independence, reaching a crucial stage. Caught between the opposing ideological forces of East and West, the African nations are seeking to draw from each those elements which will be of help to them in fashioning the new African societies while at the same time they are making every effort to maintain a position which avoids permanent alliance with either side. As a means of mutual support of their neutralist position they are groping toward a united community of African states. Yet they are finding, as their former colonial rulers found in Western Europe, that independence brings in its train impediments to unity deriving from national self-interest which even the brotherhood born of the common goal of liberation cannot as yet overcome. The break with the colonial past has been made in the greater part of the continent, but for those countries where the white man has settled, the problem remains for the African governments of reconciling the European to this new role of political impotence without losing the economic skills and resources he can bring to the aid of the new countries.

The purpose of this book is to provide a basis for discussion by presenting a point of view on four major areas of policy problems posed in Africa since independence. In much different version they were presented in 1963 as lectures in a Columbia University television series on international relations.

Certainly no attempt will be made to advance solutions to any of the questions treated; these can come only from Africans. But, by arousing the interest of the reader in pursuing these themes further, it is hoped that he will gain a deeper appreciation of the dilemmas facing the generation of Africans into whose hands the leadership of independent Africa has passed.

The material which constitutes the latter portion of the book is designed to provide some factual knowledge of the African continent and its present state of development as accurately as is possible in view of the statistics available.

It is hoped that the reader may gain through this some realization of the dimension of the task facing the African governments, and also some appreciation of the strides toward modernization that have been made in relatively a few years. The work of gathering the statistical data and of making the originals of the maps accompanying them was undertaken largely by Mrs. Annette Stiefbold, whose assistance I would like to acknowledge with deepest appreciation. For his help in the planning of the volume as a whole, my thanks are due to Robert Bass. Errors of fact and sins of misinterpretation are, unhappily, my own.

L. GRAY COWAN

New York

TABLE OF CONTENTS

Part I: Interpretation

Part II: Reference

xiii

CHAPTER ONE

The Prospect for Democracy in Africa

The Rise of African Nationalism

The nationalist revolution which swept away the European colonial empires in Africa in the two decades following World War II is part of one of the most complex political phenomena of the mid-twentieth century. By the end of 1963 the African nationalist parties had been successful in securing their major objective in almost the entire African continent. Thirty-one new countries had been created out of former colonial territories, with at least two more to appear in 1964.

In the process of securing political emancipation, the nationalist movements were forced to organize the full energies of their people to carry on the struggle. At its inception, nationalism was confined to a small minority of the educated élite who sought for their own interest a greater share in the process of government which had hitherto been the monopoly of the colonial administrations. Although there were sporadic outbreaks of resistance against the colonial regimes in the rural areas, which were led by traditionalist groups before 1945, the major impetus for the spread of nationalism came from the urban centers, where the symbols of self-government and independence could be more easily understood and communicated.

From a very early period, the urban nationalist leaders sought to forge links between the new urbanites and the rural masses. Because the city-dwellers retained a close connection to their rural homeland, the parties were able through them to transmit the message of independence to the villages. There political consciousness was gradually aroused by the young educated groups who sought more rapid political and social advancement for their peoples. Veterans who had served abroad during the war and who had received training in the armed services of the European powers became the leaders of the forces of progress which were represented by the nationalist parties. In many areas village self-help societies and tribal unions were formed to promote local improvements; these, too, in time became the nuclei of nationalist organization because in them were focused the grievances of the more politically conscious rural minority.

The spread of nationalism inevitably met with resistance from the colonial administrations. Where the administration sought to suppress the nationalist organization of a formal political party, alternative sources of collective strength were found. The trade union movement was one of these, providing as it did experience in organization and leadership as well as ideological orientation. Other bodies such as the syncretistic churches, which were the purely African offshoots of the churches established by the European missions, and women's groups and youth groups, organized for social or athletic purposes, served as vehicles to carry the nationalists' message. At every level of society, nationalism became an integrating symbol for all shades of political opinion.

In bringing their message to the people, the nationalist parties used techniques of party organization and discipline which the leaders had learned abroad, both in Europe and in the United States. Particularly in French-speaking Africa, the Marxist-Leninist prescriptions for mass appeal through a highly disciplined and tightly organized cellular party fell upon receptive ears. Inevitably this type of party led to a heavy emphasis on the personality of the man who was able to make himself the leader of the movement. To be a successful leader meant that he had to possess organizing skill and political acumen in dealing with colonial officials but, above all, personal magnetism or charisma which would enable him to gather behind him the support of the masses, for whose political ambitions he became the spokesman. In part, too, he became a substitute for the traditional authority to which the people were accustomed at the village level and for which no equivalent existed at the new level of the national unit. To some extent all the leaders of the nationalist groups in Africa possessed these qualities of charisma, although a few, such as Kwame Nkrumah of Ghana or Jomo Kenyatta of Kenya, may be singled out for the exceptional degree to which they owe their present positions of leadership to them.

The major task of the early nationalist parties was the establishment of a coherent structure to provide close links from the party hierarchy gathered about the leader down to the lowest unit of the village committee. Typically, this meant a political bureau or national executive committee whose decisions were transmitted through party sections which frequently corresponded to the administrative divisions of the country. The sections, in turn, were the points of articulation between the upper national level of the party and the rural villages. Through the sections, party discipline and coordination were maintained. The village committees were responsible for the spread of detailed knowledge of party policy and, in addition, they were used as sounding boards to insure that party policy remained in touch with popular opinion. The platform of the nationalist parties prior to independence was simple and direct—self-government and independence; all the efforts of party followers were directed toward this end. Moreover, the platform's inclusiveness left little room for opposition. Those who failed to agree with this goal were inevitably branded as traitors to the interests of the masses. Political leaders who refused to join the dominant nationalist group had little upon which to base an appeal to the people, since no real alternative could be offered.

In any case, the party which had captured the leadership of the nationalist movement concentrated within its hands virtually all political activity, making it exceedingly difficult for an opposition party to duplicate its organization. Such opposition as did exist during this early period tended to form on a sectional or tribal basis. This, for instance, was the case in Ashanti in Ghana, but here as elsewhere it had little hope of gaining over-all national support. During the formative period of African parties, then, the establishment of a real opposition party in most states was made almost impossible because of the colonial situation within which the dominant nationalist party arose. If there can be said to have been an opposition, it was embodied in the colonial government itself, since it was against the policies of the administration that the nationalists directed their energies. The real role of an opposition in the parliamentary sense was never made clear before independence simply because there was no place for it in the political spectrum.

Despite the occasional disturbances which took place during the nationalist campaigns between 1945 and 1960, in the vast majority of cases the culmination of the struggle for independence was reached without serious violence. Often, independence came, not in consequence of pitched battles which sought to wrest power from the hands of a reluctant colonial authority, but rather in the form of a grant of independence made in such a way as to make the nationalist struggle appear to be somewhat anticlimactic. Except in Algeria, Kenya and the Cameroon Republic, the birth of independence was not accompanied by violence entailing any substantial loss of life. Even in the Congo, the violence which took place in July, 1960, was actually a consequence of the post-independence breakdown of public authority.

However peaceful the final act of surrender of the colonial power may have been, the major nationalist parties were almost everywhere so well organized that in the last pre-independence elections they were swept into power with overwhelming majorities. There was little or no cleavage of opinion on the issue of self-rule, nor was a great deal of public attention given to the policies proposed by the dominant party for the post-independence period. The nationalist program, insofar as it was really articulated at all, simply reflected the ideological predilections of the leadership of the party. Thus, for example, in Guinea, the political style of the new government showed strong elements of Sekou Touré's interpretation of Marx. In Nigeria, on the other hand, the ideological views of the leaders of the coalition parties that formed the first independent federal government were comparatively much more conservative and also more Western-oriented.

The independent governments saw as their earliest tasks the promotion of national unity and the raising of living standards. The first of these was the more pressing, since political solidarity and stability were the prerequisites for any genuine economic advance. The geographical units over which the new governments were to rule were in every case essentially artificial creations carved out of Africa by the colonial powers in the late nineteenth century. Only rarely had the European administrations paid much attention to ethnic considerations in delineating the new frontiers. Yet the new leaders felt compelled to create a sense of national identity within the existing frontiers simply because their appeal to their peoples had been based on independence for the Nigeria, the Ghana or the Guinea which had existed on the map. To try to change the existing borders would only increase the divisive forces inherent in long-standing tribal enmities which in some countries already threatened to destroy the new nation.

The national political parties sought to minimize the effects of these forces by exploiting the wave of enthusiasm which accompanied independence. To reinforce the sense of national community as well as to give the individual citizen a sense of participation in the great work of national development, self-help schemes — known as "human investment" — were organized, frequently based on the same tribal societies that had served earlier as party nuclei. The enormous reservoir of collective energy which had been marshaled for the independence struggle had now to be channeled into activities which would produce the concrete improvement in the lives of the people which had been promised as the aftermath of political independence.

The tasks facing the new governments were staggering. The day-to-day problems of administration were complicated by the departure of many key colonial administrators, and even to keep a bare minimum of governmental services in operation men with little or no experience were called upon to replace them. Even in countries such as Nigeria, where preparation for independence had been under way for some years, Africanization of the civil service was far from complete and whole new departments of government, such as the Foreign Ministry, had to be manned immediately. The governments were called upon immediately to make decisions on both internal and external policies for which virtually no planning had been done.

Confronted by circumstances and pressures coincident with independence, it is not surprising that the leaders of the African states found little time to reflect on the establishment of the democratic process and on the place of an opposition in the domestic political spectrum.

The Political Pattern of Independence

Somewhat to the disappointment of the European colonial powers and the West in general, the new African states have not radically altered the pattern of political party activity established in the years before independence. The Western-style institutions of parliamentary government created in British and French Africa were in many countries eclipsed by the continuing phenomenon of the single party. While it might have been expected that the African states would initially have difficulties in operating the governmental structures deeded them by the colonial powers, the former rulers were hardly prepared for the frequently expressed view of many African leaders that such institutions were neither suitable for the African countries at this stage of their development nor likely to be in the foreseeable future. Instead, Africans insisted that, while they might build on some parts of the European foundation, their ultimate goal was to devise institutions which would be more suited to the African conception of the functions of government and which would correspond more closely to the traditional African style of political decision-making. The single-party system which was the product of the mold into which nationalist politics fitted prior to independence was thus carried over into post-nationalist politics to the point where it has become the single most characteristic feature of the contemporary African political scene.

The Single-Party Structure

With a few major exceptions (such as Nigeria and Kenya) single parties dominate the governments of all the new African states. They are for the most part those parties which came to power at independence and have many of the same leaders who were most active in the earlier nationalist period. These are the parties which were able to construct the most effective organizational networks before independence and which have been able to maintain wide national support through their local branches since. Although they go through the motions of periodic elections, there is no effective opposition in an institutionalized form and hence such elections serve only as a method of reaffirming the solidarity of the nation behind the existing leadership.

African arguments supporting the single-party system are based on both pragmatic and theoretical grounds. The pragmatic justification derives from the view that in the crisis following independence a strong government is needed to weld the nation together. The needs of economic develop-

7

ment are imperative and evident; there can be no argument about goals and therefore parties representing different points of view are superfluous. The single party, it is claimed, represents the will of all the people. It permits mass participation in decision-making and in so doing encourages the development of a sense of personal responsibility in government. Moreover, since it does not represent only the interests of a group, a section or an economic class in the population, it is basically more democratic than the Western multi-party system.

Madeira Keita, an official of the Union Sudanaise, the governing party of Mali, stated the case clearly in an article published in 1960 in which he pointed out: "In the present historical situation in Africa there is no need to multiply parties, nor to indulge in the luxury of a sterile and fratricidal opposition. Since we were agreed on the essentials and were pursuing the same objectives, was there any reason to remain divided and split into parties that fought one another?" But M. Keita also recognized that the single-party system is not without its dangers. "But how to safeguard the ideals of liberty and democracy in the single party? ... Democracy is the exercise of public authority in conformance with the will of the masses. . . . If there is one party it is necessary, first of all, that it be the true expression of the aspirations of the people. . . . This is only possible to the degree that the party is solidly organized and there is real discipline within the party so that decisions are taken only after lengthy debate and free discussion . . . the system of the unified party demands more honesty, more disinterest and more devotion from the leadership. . . . One can remain a leader in Africa for a long time only if one is really acting effectively."[1]

Western critics of the single-party system in Africa have argued that instead of promoting democracy it has given rise to dictatorships which refuse to permit the forma-

[1]Keita's text is reprinted in Paul Sigmund (ed.), *The Ideologies of the Developing Nations* (New York: Praeger, 1963), pp. 170-82. Quotations are from the editor's translations.

tion of an opposition party, or in those few cases where an opposition exists, have not permitted it to play its rightful role as the continuing critic of government policy. It does not necessarily follow, however, that the future of democracy in Africa would have been more assured had the African majority parties allowed full rein to opposition parties within a parliamentary structure. Underlying the argument for an opposition is the implicit assumption that a Western-modeled parliament is applicable to all societies regardless of their cultural background.

·In those African states where opposition parties were permitted to exercise their prerogative freely after independence, it rapidly became clear that the concept of the "loyal opposition" was by no means clear to the opposition leaders. They appear to have felt that their role was not that of offering constructive criticism but rather of seeking the downfall of the government by being as destructive as possible. There is certainly some truth in the complaints of the majority party leadership that the opposition regarded its chief function as that of hampering the government in carrying out any policy whatever, nor did the opposition feel that the onus of providing alternatives to the programs it criticized fell upon its shoulders.

While there is no doubt that some governments, such as that in Ghana, have repressed opposition movements beyond any point justified by the opposition's activities, there is no proof that the opposition, had it been in the same position, would have acted differently. All too often the opposition leaders have made it apparent that their goal in seeking office is for the sake of power alone (to the point where they have not hesitated to seek to overthrow the government by force if they felt that an appeal to the voters would fail) and not to provide better solutions to the problems of government.

In a recent speech, President Julius Nyerere of Tanganyika made the point that it was of vital importance that in a new state the institutions of government be understood by the people. If they are not, they cannot hope to encourage national unity. Nyerere's point is well taken. The Western nations — Britain, the United States, France and others — have taken generations to develop those political institutions which they feel will best serve the needs of their societies, and the process is by no means finished. The parliaments, and the parliamentary forms devised by Britain and France and deeded to the colonies in Africa, were developed as a felt response over the course of centuries to the needs of European societies. It is not to be expected that these institutions will always meet the needs of African societies, whose traditions and backgrounds differ from our own. President Nyerere went on to add that for his own country:

> There must be no confusing outward forms which are meaningless in the light of our own experience in history. This alone requires a Republic, and one with an executive President.
> To us, honor and respect are accorded to a Chief, Monarch, or a President, not because of his symbolism but because of the authority and responsibility he holds. We are not used to the division between real authority and formal authority.
> The President must not only carry the responsibility for the actions of Government, he must have the power to fulfill his responsibilities. . . . The Government are aware that some of our friends may be overconscious of the dangers of dictatorship, but they recognise an overriding need to provide leadership.
> We have to acknowledge that although the people of Tanganyika can understand the idea of law being made by groups, they see leadership and the enforcement of the law as the responsibility of a person, with authority, answerable for his actions to the group but not hampered by it in effecting them. Under our proposals therefore, where it is necessary to lead, the President has the powers to lead.[2]

President Nyerere went on to emphasize, however, that within this structure of the strong Executive, Parliament must remain sovereign and expressive of the will of the people. Yet the sovereignty of Parliament does not, in his view, necessarily mean the existence within it of a two-party

[2]Quoted in *Africa Report*, July, 1962, p. 5.

system since, as he contends, "Where one party is identified with a nation as a whole, the foundations of democracy are firmer than they can ever be when you have two or more parties, each representing only a section of the community." While he recognizes that the checks and balances provided by the party system and those built into the constitution in the American presidential system are necessary to preserve democracy in a developed country, in the case of the African nations such a system of brakes on social change is unnecessary. "Our need is not for brakes — our lack of trained manpower and capital resources, and even our climate, act too effectively already. We need accelerators powerful enough to overcome the inertia bred of poverty, and the resistance, which are inherent in all societies."

The Western parliamentary structure is, then, in the view of many African leaders, an alien institution with no roots in African society. Most African tribal political systems provided methods for limited popular participation in political decision-making. Few, if any, African rulers governed as autocrats; usually they were surrounded by councils of some type without whose consent no important decisions could be taken. In many instances, formal provisions were made for an expression of popular opinion concerning the replacement of a Chief, or members of his council, who transgressed tribal mores seriously. But these provisions did not involve expressions of majority and minority opinion tabulated as individual votes. One anthropologist comments on this point: "I have never found it recorded . . . that the Council of Elders, or clan leaders, settled important issues by formal vote, with the will of the majority prevailing. Evidently, the idea of basing a group decision on a vote is not as self-evident as we usually assume, or else it is incompatible with other values in African cultures which are more deeply entrenched."[3]

Anyone who has witnessed traditional African village meetings will be aware of the strong inclination at this

[3] Robert F. Grey, "Political Parties in New African Nations: An Anthropological View," *Comparative Studies in Society and History*, IV., No. 4 (July 19, 1963), pp. 451-2.

level of African politics toward consensus democracy. Even where, in contemporary English-speaking Africa, British-modeled elected councils at the village and district level are expected to carry on their business on the basis of the parliamentary strictures of *Robert's Rules of Order,* every effort is made to avoid posing a question in such a way as to contrast sharply opposing views to the point where it is necessary to decide the question by majority vote. The African method of arriving at a decision is to discuss the matter at what may seem at times inordinate length, and during the discussion to give everyone concerned a chance to express his opinion as fully as possible. At a point difficult for the outsider to discern, a consensus is reached which is shared by all those present, thus obviating the necessity of a vote, which would leave the community sharply split. The device of a "committee of the whole," permissible under *Robert's Rules,* allows for this free discussion preliminary to a consensus, and the formal vote on the question, taken for the council records, is, as a result, invariably unanimous. Thus it is possible to combine the African consensus method with the more formalistic rules of Western procedure in a way which satisfies the demands of both worlds. To quote Professor Grey again:

> When issues between opposing parties are decided ultimately by parliamentary vote, it leaves the outvoted minority with its will or desire unsatisfied. A whole society must exist for indefinite periods of time knowing that some of its members, who may represent a considerable proportion, do not favor the political action being pursued, but have only agreed to restrain their active opposition for the time being. . . . The usual procedure of parliamentary voting makes it inevitable that at all times, part of the society will remain in unsatisfied opposition to important decisions affecting the whole society. This implication of parliamentary vote is evidently not in accord with African political ideals.[4]

While the form of the village consensus cannot be carried over entirely into the realm of national government, nevertheless the African traditional method of reaching

[4]*Ibid.,* p. 457.

12

public decisions has made it more difficult to institutionalize the existence of continuing opposition in the legislatures inherited from the colonial period.

The outside world has been prompt to lay the blame for what appears to be the growing political instability of the African states at the door of the one-party system. The argument is that the attempts by the governing parties to satisfy all sections of their populations have not been successful. The dissatisfactions engendered have led to such frustrations on the part of the opposition, which has had no legitimate outlet for its grievances, that they have culminated in repeated attempts to overthrow the governments by force. So endemic have these attempts become that a prominent African newspaper had, in mid-1963, begun to run a column entitled "The Plot of the Week."

The succession of plots aimed at overthrowing the governments in such countries as Togo and Dahomey, where they were successful, and in Ghana and Nigeria, where they failed, exposed the African single parties to the charge that in their haste to legitimize themselves and to push ahead with national development they have only laid the foundation for chronic instability.

In some degree, a part of the instability which plagues many African states is the result of a clash between the Western-inspired parliamentary system and the indigenous consensus democracy. But the new African states suffer also from a built-in instability which derives fundamentally from the rapid process of modernization. The rise of nationalism, the drive toward independence, and finally the stage of independence itself have profoundly shaken the foundations of African society. The vast movement of population from rural to urban areas, the spread of education and technical training, and the change from a barter to a money economy have combined to create for many millions of Africans a world in which new anticipations and ambitions may be realized but which at the same time has within it complexities and uncertainties that were never faced in traditional

13

society. In government many new types of authority have come into being: one day a man may be a farmer in his field, and almost the next day, a Member of Parliament, or a Minister. The expansion and Africanization of the bureaucracy have created new decision-makers, and positions of influence at the local community level have sprung up within the hierarchy of the nationalist parties. Economic development has created new roles for the African entrepreneur out of which grow ever more complex patterns of roles which combine the authority of the new wealth with that of a high position within the political party. The foundations of a highly stratified and multi-dimensional modern society are slowly being laid alongside a structure of traditional society which has by no means lost its vitality. The conflicts between the authority resulting from these new roles and that from traditional roles, and the jockeying for power which is an inevitable part of the still-limited opportunities offered to the growing educated élite, create a social instability which becomes readily reflected in the political process.

In a recent study of modernization in Burma, Lucian Pye argues that the psychological challenge and response presented by the whole process of modernization and Westernization is in itself a cause of political instability.[5] No matter what their education, or the degree to which they have been acculturated to a Western tradition, the leaders of many of the new states have deep, underlying doubts as to whether they (or their people) can, in the last analysis, measure up to the challenge of a modern technological world. The insecurity bred of this lingering doubt of the ability to achieve modernization provides a rationale for continued control of the political process through the single-party system. In Africa, Kwame Nkrumah of Ghana has argued that the economic independence which gives substance to political independence can be achieved only by the welding of national unity. Respect for the new nations of Africa, he insists, will only come in the international community when

---

[5] *Politics, Personality and Nation Building* (New Haven, Yale University Press, 1963).

they have proved that they are capable of competing as modern states with the states of the more developed parts of the world. To insure the full mobilization of society behind the drive to create a new nation, a high degree of control in the immediate post-independence period is necessary. Under the psychological pressure resulting from the often overly ambitious goals of the leaders, the nationalist party becomes increasingly impatient of criticism and of what it considers obstructive tactics, and in the process, even genuinely constructive critics may find themselves the victims of a Preventive Detention Act. Unfortunately, the leaders have given little consideration to the possible long-range consequences of the loss of individual liberty which the drive for national identification entails. Their aim, as they see it, is to proceed as rapidly as possible with the transformation of society while trying to keep in check those forces of dislocation created in the process so as to prevent them from tearing asunder the very framework of the society itself.

It is this precarious process of balancing change against stability that often presents a confusing picture of African politics to the outside world. African leaders may make public statements designed for an external audience which conflict with, or even directly contradict, actions taken within the context of the domestic political situation. President Nkrumah's role as a world statesman and as president of his country requires a very different political posture from his role as leader of the Convention People's Party (CPP). Yet his actions in both roles are often treated by the foreign press as proceeding from the same set of motivations, and he, as well as other African leaders, is therefore accused of failing to live up to standards of public conduct which, in their own eyes, are not applicable in a period of such fundamental change as that taking place in Africa today.

Stability and Democracy

While there may be some validity to Nyerere's argument that a strong form of government is necessary for

Africa at this stage, and that it corresponds to the desire of the majority of the people, the fact cannot be brushed aside that experience over the past five years has indicated that a strong Executive may well assume dictatorial characteristics in his haste to achieve the economic progress which is so frequently seen as the prime necessity. The tragedy of contemporary Africa is that the urgency of the need to release the brakes on social change has all too often led to the personalization of power. It can, of course, be argued that in the colonial period power in Africa was personalized in the hands of the Governor, whose position had a generous element of authoritarianism built into it. Yet in the last analysis his powers were never absolute and there was always recourse to the higher authority of London. Clearly there is always danger inherent in placing full constitutional authority in the hands of one man even for a temporary period. The degree of danger, however, depends on the personality of the individual in whom the powers are vested. In the case of President Nyerere of Tanganyika, the powers are granted with the full consent of the people, and should this consent be withdrawn, there is every probability that he would step down without demur. Here, then, the risk may be taken with a certain impunity. On the other hand, if the personality of the leader is such that the possession of power becomes for him an end in itself without regard to popular consent, he will clearly resist surrender of that power to the point where he can only be displaced by an act of violence. The delusion of omnipotence can frequently be far more perilous to the state than the personal exercise of supreme power in a period of national crisis such as prevails in many African states today.

The personalized power exercised by some African heads of state may deeply affect the future development of the African nations because it acts to prevent the establishment of an accepted and legitimized method for transferring power from one leader to another. One of the cornerstones of long-term political stability in any system is the institutionalization of methods of leadership change. In traditional Africa, authority was vested in the position of the Chief, and not in the man. However absolute his powers may have been as Chief, procedures for the selection of his successor were generally recognized by his people as part of the traditional political system. While it is true that these procedures did not always work smoothly and the selection of a new Chief gave rise to much strife within the community, nevertheless such bickering seldom threatened to undermine the basic stability of the system. In Africa today, the national units are too new to have established popularly accepted rules for the succession of power. The leaders who brought the country to independence are still in office in most cases; where they have been removed forcibly from the scene, a period of crisis has frequently ensued until new leaders could effectively seize the reins of power. Although all the new African states have constitutional provisions for governmental succession, these provisions have for the most part not yet been tested. In any case, there is serious question whether any constitutional procedures can be really effective in the single-party system unless the leader has been in a position to designate his successor in such a way as to satisfy all factions within the party. Paradoxically, the greater the power of the leader, the more difficult is the task of designating a successor acceptable to the party as a whole. Inevitably, if the line of succession is made too evident during the leader's lifetime, he runs the risk of permanently alienating certain groups within his own party who expect the successor to be chosen from among their members; or the successor-designate may become too impatient to wait for his predecessor to turn over the reins of power and may force the succession prematurely. The problem of leadership succession in one-party systems is, of course, by no means confined to African states: it is a phenomenon common to all countries where this type of political system prevails. Succession does, however, become a peculiarly acute problem in African states where the foundations of a national political community are only just being laid.

To avoid the dilemma of choice between personalized leadership and political continuity attempts have been made in some African states to establish the primacy of the party over the state itself and to create popular acceptance of a party ideology (which may very well represent the ideology of the present leader only) that will provide for continuity regardless of who may become the next party leader. Ghana and Guinea provide two examples of countries in which the creation and dissemination of a party ideology have been most heavily stressed. The ideological bases for party action which have been constructed by Sekou Touré in Guinea for his Parti Démocratique de Guinée, and by Kwame Nkrumah for the Convention People's Party in Ghana, are designed to provide the broad framework for party policies which will lead to the goals of social and economic development postulated by the party leadership. They provide not only a rationale for party action today, but the foundations upon which future policies may be based.

Both the political philosophy of Sekou Touré in Guinea and "Nkrumahism" in Ghana draw heavily on Marxian doctrine for inspiration. Although the ideologies of both parties derive from Marx and from European socialism, Nkrumahism lays heavy emphasis on the adaptation of socialism to the peculiar needs and conditions of Africa. According to one definition, Nkrumahism is "a non-atheistic socialist philosophy which seeks to apply the current socialist ideas to the solution of our problems, be they domestic or international, by adapting these ideas to the realities of everyday life."[6] But Nkrumahism is not, in the view of its proponents, socialism in the European sense of the term.

> In order to distinguish it from socialism in other places, which in its entirety may not be suitable or applicable to the conditions and circumstances in Africa, it has been described as "African socialism." This should not be interpreted to mean a restriction of its application only to Africa; it only means that as a socialist non-doctrinaire

[6]Kofi Baako, "Nkrumahism, Its Theory and Practice," *The Party* (CPP Journal), April, 1961, p. 3.

philosophy it is primarily designed to solve the peculiar social, economic, and political problems imposed by imperialism and colonialism on our continent. . . . It has definite content and objective, namely, a social reform aimed at the abolition of the social power wielded by private capital property and replacing it with the social power held by the people through the State. . . . This presupposes the establishment of a socio-economic structure which insures not a mere redistribution of property but a just distribution of income out of the yield of the socio-economic process with the aim of a proportionate distribution of property.[7]

Nkrumah's view that socialism as defined by Marx and Lenin must be interpreted by Africans to suit African needs is shared by Léopold Senghor, the President of Senegal, who insists: "Our socialism can no longer be exactly like that of Marx and Engels which was elaborated about a hundred years ago, according to the scientific methods and circumstances of the nineteenth century and Western Europe."[8] Sekou Touré and Nkrumah both have argued that a form of socialism, whatever its source, is better suited to Africa because the African traditional village system was communalistic — "A society in which the welfare of the individual is bound up with the welfare of all the people in the community — and therefore more akin to socialism than is the Western individualistic philosophy of capitalism." Socialism is not, however, regarded as an abstract doctrine to be practiced for its own sake, since to do so would, in Touré's words, be "to try to reap only with the handle of the sickle" but rather as a tool by which the material standards of living of the people may be raised.

The philosophy of the Parti Démocratique de Guinée, however, as expressed by Sekou Touré, differs from both Nkrumah and Senghor in that Touré disagrees that there can be any modification of socialist doctrine purely in terms of an application of this doctrine to Africa. There is, in fact, in Touré's view, no such doctrine as "African" socialism; such a distinction he believes to be a contradiction in terms.

[7] *Ibid.*, p. 4.
[8] Speech at Conference on African Socialism, Dakar, December, 1962.

"In Africa a good deal is heard about African socialism which would seem to mean, apparently, that there exists a Chinese socialism or an American socialism, a Yugoslavian or Bulgarian socialism. If a political theory is to be thus defined in the abstract, nothing will stop us tomorrow from speaking of the Nigerian or the Congolese roads to the building of African socialism." With varying degrees of commitment, socialism is nevertheless seen by most African parties as the form of economic organization best suited to meeting the needs of their peoples, whether or not it has a specifically African flavor. The argument that socialism is more compatible with the traditionally communal African form of village life than is the individual-initiative type of organization of Western capitalism seems debatable. The life of the farmer within the economic structure of the African village, and the life of the worker in an urban industrial setting, are so dissimilar as to make comparison dangerous.

One element of attraction in socialism for contemporary African leaders is that they see it as a non-Western doctrine. The Leninist explanation of the causes of imperialism has always found substantial agreement among the colonial nationalists both in Asia and in Africa. Western capitalism is frequently equated with those aspects of imperialism they regard as exploitative. By definition, Marxist-Leninist socialism cannot be imperialist and is therefore seen as more acceptable.

More generally, however, socialism is regarded throughout the developing world as a progressive force as contrasted to capitalism. For the modernizing nationalists, socialism represents an ideology designed to promote the development of the national economy for the good of the people as a whole, not for the profit of a minority. The egalitarian content of socialism in its advocacy of a common share in the national product fits in closely with the nationalists' goal of equal treatment of the African in every sphere of life.

Despite the emphasis on the social ownership of the major means of production, the socialism advocated by the African leadership in most countries leaves considerable scope for the continued private ownership of many industrial facilities and a real place in the economy for the private entrepreneur. This element of Nkrumahism is stressed by Kofi Baako:

> Nkrumahism does not aim at the abolition of personal ownership of your own personal property—such as your house, your farm, your car, your frigidaire or property which you or your family may possess. The individual citizen or inhabitant is encouraged to work for an income commensurate with the work he does and is free to use his income to satisfy his existential requirements—provided that he does not use what he has to foster an exploitation of man by man.[9]

The pragmatic strain which is so much a part of the theoretical pronouncements on socialism in Africa derives in part from the awareness on the part of African political leaders of the strong inclination toward private initiative which is to be seen everywhere in the African trading community and also from an awareness of the continuing necessity on the part of most African economies for development capital which must in many areas come from private outside sources. Although much of the planning and the execution of industrial development will for some time to come remain in the hands of government, no African government is prepared, for reasons of theoretical socialism, to reject the aid which can come from Western private capital.

The concepts that are being formulated under the general term "African socialism" are as yet frequently vague, incomplete and even contradictory. The fact that they contain elements both of Marxian Communism and of Western capitalism reflects the strong desire of the African leadership to evolve a third position of neutrality between the two major contending ideological forces in the world. Thus their political theory corresponds to the non-alignment which has become their stance in foreign policy. From each

---

[9] *Op. cit.*, p. 4.

of the two ideologies they seek to choose those concepts which will be most useful as a result of a pragmatic evaluation of their own future needs. Sekou Touré has repeatedly pointed out that foreign observers of Guinea have failed to distinguish in the doctrine of the PDG between the use of Marxist-Leninist prescriptions for political party organization and the adoption of Marxism as a total political philosophy. It is evident that the Guinean party is modeled closely on that of the Soviet Union in its highly stratified but closely interlocking structure which comprises branches on every level of Guinean society. This aspect of Marxist teaching has been found useful for social mobilization, but it does not follow that this mobilization is necessarily aimed at the same ends as those foreseen by Marx. The African socialists diverge at several points from some of the basic elements of Marxism. Touré has denied, for example, that the doctrine of the class struggle is valid for Africa today because no African country has an industrial proletariat. Touré specifically denies the anti-religious teachings of Marx on the ground that religion has traditionally been basic to the African community and that Africans could not accept a philosophy based only on materialistic values.

Despite the present somewhat confusing eclecticism of the African leaders, it is gradually becoming clear that heavy emphasis will be laid in the African political systems on those values which tend to solidify and integrate the community and less upon the individualism which is conceived to be a characteristic of the Western community. In consequence, therefore, there will tend to be less concern with civil liberties and the protection of the individual under the rule of law than the West is accustomed to. Within the traditional African village, the rights of the individual, as well as his privileges, were regarded as distinctly secondary to those of the community and the family. The individual who, by his actions, endangered the solidarity or the continued existence of his extended family and of the families who made up the community rendered himself liable to the ultimate sanction, that of being cast out of the group. His life depended on the support of those around him; in turn they claimed the right to prescribe, often very narrowly, the confines of his liberties as an individual. The new community of the nation state is only now in the process of creation. Its foundations are fragile and the consensus upon which it is being built is not always secure. Acts which threaten this consensus threaten the state and will be harshly judged by the new leaders, more particularly so if they appear to favor the interests of an individual or a group to the detriment of the people as a whole. So long as the leadership feels itself engaged in the struggle for legitimization of its existence, and even for the existence of the nation itself, it will continue to insist upon guidance, direction and control by a modernizing élite; they, not the individual, will set the norms of social conduct.

Against this trend toward strong, centralized guidance there is, however, arising in the African states a countervailing force which may in the long run have the effect of molding the new governments in greater degree along the more familiar lines of Western democracy. For the developed Western nations, particularly the United States, an aspect of the democratic system which is of importance equal to or even greater than the multi-party system is the requirement that any government pursue policies which effect compromises among the wide variety of competing economic interest groups existing in a modern economy. No American party could afford to pursue policies which consistently favored the manufacturing group or the agricultural group, or any of their varied sub-sections, to the exclusion of other interest groups. Such a Government would lose the confidence of a large mass of the people in very short order. The only viable policies, therefore, are those which satisfy the interests of as many groups as possible, or at least satisfy their interests in part. If one policy decision goes far to meet the interests of one group, it must be counterweighted by a decision which goes equally far to meet the interests of another group or groups. The interests of smaller groups may be ignored by the Government for a time but one of the major objectives of any group is to gather enough adherents behind it to be able to apply effective pressure to the lawmakers so that its particular interest will receive consideration. It is, then, upon this balancing of competitive group interests that the successful operation of American or Western European democracy substantially rests.

In the new African states, as elsewhere in the developing world, one of the major difficulties is the absence of differentiated economic interest groups. Compared to the developed countries of the West, African societies today tend to be relatively undifferentiated in terms of these interest groups, although they may be highly differentiated along traditional or other lines of social stratification. Many groups within the African states at the present stage of development are not organized in such a way as to be capable of applying effective pressure to the new governments since they frequently represent traditional or at least non-modernizing forces which involve the interests of decreasing numbers of the population. The economic interest of the vast majority of the African population, the peasant farmers, remains largely unarticulated through lack of organization whereby to press its demands on government. But in all African countries there is rapidly growing an urban population whose economic interests are much more sharply focused and which possesses the ability through education to demand satisfaction of its interests from the government. The voice of such urban groups has been and will continue to be, in part, the labor unions.

With industrialization there are beginning to grow up other economic interests at a number of levels: those of management, the retailer, the distributor and even the investor. So far the business communities of most African states are relatively small, and their activities may be restricted in the degree to which the government is pursuing a policy of state ownership of production facilities. But the private sector of the economy in such large countries as Nigeria is starting to wield influence sufficient so that its interests cannot be ignored.

Although it may be expected that the major source of new interest groups in the African states will be gradually increasing economic differentiation, there are other groups whose origins stem from the changes in African society arising from the creation of independent states. While no attempt can be made here to indicate all or even a small number of the new groups which are potentially of political importance in the new governments, a few may be singled out for particular attention.

One of the most important of these may come to be the military group. The nucleus of a military establishment existed in most of the African colonies prior to independence. In the case of the ex-British colonies of Africa, the West African Regiment dates back many years, and in French Africa, the famous Senegalese troops were used by the mother country in both world wars. But an important difference between the post-independence military establishment and the earlier one is that today the military is under the control of an African government and is commanded by African rather than by European officers of the former colonial power. As a potential political interest group, the military officers of the new African countries are of enormous importance. Not only do they have technical training and a high degree of education, but the men they command represent, along with the police, a disciplined and organized force which could be used to influence the civilian Government, or in an extreme case, to overthrow the civilian power completely. In most African countries, the military has thus far been prepared to accept control by the legitimately elected Government. Yet there have been a sufficient number of cases in which military action has been used to displace the civilian Government so as to illustrate amply how effective the threat of military interference with the normal processes of government can be. Perhaps the outstanding example is that of the revolt in the Congo shortly after independence in 1960, but other and less spectacular examples of the rise of the military are not difficult to find. The army was responsible for the changes in the regime in Dahomey in 1963, and indirectly for the assassination of President Olympio of Togo, in 1962. In a number of other countries, the military has been accused of at least conniving at plots to overturn the legitimately elected authority. In the case of Senegal in December, 1962, it was the support of the armed forces which decided the struggle between the President, Léopold Senghor, and the Prime Minister, Mamadou Dia, in favor of Senghor. In the Sudan, the military has been the effective government for some years past.

So long as the civilian authority remains strong enough to direct the affairs of state in a reasonably satisfactory manner, and so long as the government maintains a reasonable degree of stability, the threat of a military coup remains slight. But in those cases where civilian control is weakened through party bickering, or where there exists the threat of paralysis of the democratic process and exposure to a possible take-over by a Communist front, or when the government is clearly unable to meet at least a modicum of the demands of the military, there remains the possibility that the military will decide to use the force it commands to right the situation. There is a strong desire on the part of the military to prove its professional respectability not only in the eyes of its own people but in the eyes of other nations as well. Where the military is convinced that the national honor of the country or its image abroad is being denigrated by the inefficiency or inaction of the civilian government it may well decide to take matters into its own hands.

Another growing interest group which no African government today can afford to ignore entirely is the youth of the country. In some countries, notably Nigeria, where the now older generation of nationalist leaders who are in power have failed to provide the post-independence opportunities which the youth groups had been led to expect, the possibility has existed of the youth leadership forming its own political party, based on a much more radical platform than that offered by the older nationalist parties. Within the single-party system, the party leadership has had, as in Ghana, at least to make gestures toward the satisfaction of the demands of youth. In Nigeria the regionalism of the party structure has not yet become sufficiently weakened to permit the formation of a national youth party, although such a possibility cannot be excluded from the future of Nigerian politics. Discontent among the youth groups tends to be concentrated in the graduates, for whom the economy has not developed fast enough to offer urban industrial jobs, and in the lower branches of the civil service, where opportunity is now sharply limited because of the relative youthfulness of those occupying the senior posts.

In some African countries, religions or traditional authorities continue to function as interest groups. In Senegal, for example, factions within the Moslem faith had, even before independence, acted as effective pressure groups, and their influence is still felt as a political factor in post-independence politics. Although the role of the traditional Chiefs will undoubtedly continue to grow smaller with the continued process of modernization, they nevertheless constitute a focus of authority with which the nationalist governments have had to deal both before and since independence. In some areas, such as Western Nigeria, the cooperation of the traditional authorities was essential to the development of the political party. After independence, the continued support of the Chiefs was an essential element in the maintenance of local party organizational solidarity. In the early years of the nationalist movements, the Chiefs were frequently regarded as brakes on progress, and the goal of many nationalists was to discard them as soon as conveniently possible. Since independence, however, in many countries the position of the Chief has been undergoing a re-evaluation, and gradually a greater emphasis is being laid on his symbolic role as one of the foundations upon which

African society is built. Through the figure of the Chief the new political parties can emphasize the cultural uniqueness of Africa, and in him they can demonstrate the continuity which unites pre-colonial Africa with modern-day independent Africa. Through the Chief and his traditional counselors the young educated élite of today can make more concrete the relationship between the cultural values of the African past which they have emphasized in the "African personality," and the new non-African values which the process of modernization is inevitably bringing to African society.

The appearance of increasing numbers of groups whose interests are often in direct conflict has begun to pose a serious problem for the future existence of the one-party system. No government in a modern, complex society can be all things to all men at all times. Thus far the single parties deriving from the pre-independence period have been able to conserve sufficient flexibility in their platforms to be able to take account of the interests of the major groups in society. The needs for development have been so urgent at all levels of the economy that, provided general progress toward meeting them was made, the demands of minor special interest groups could be largely absorbed, or ignored. But, as the number of groups with varied interests grows, increasing strain is put on the single party to contain conflicting demands. In the not too distant future in some of the more advanced countries sizable groups may begin to feel that their demands can only be met by radical alteration of the party's policies, or, if this fails, by formation of a new party which will serve more directly to express their needs. The attempt to alter the platform of the governing party can result in temporary disruption of the political process or even in violence if the attempt is resisted by a still comparatively strong old-guard leadership. If, however, the structure of the single party has been weakened by too long an enjoyment of the fruits of power it may very well be unable to resist the efforts of a group of supporters to break away and a two-party or multi-party system may result.

The commitment of the present party leaders in Africa to the need for a single party will undoubtedly make the creation of second parties both long and arduous; in all countries it will require a period of years, and in some it may never come about at all. But it is difficult to resist the view that the very elements of the modernizing revolution through which the African states are now so rapidly passing do not in themselves contain, in the long run, the seeds of destruction of today's single parties. The replacement of the personalized and often authoritarian aspects of the new African governments with the checks and balances of a Western multi-party parliamentary system will perhaps not take place within this generation. Yet the foundations of democracy are slowly being laid. The structure will not be completed without false starts and alterations of the plans. But we in the West might remember that we have not yet completed the building of democracy to our own satisfaction; there may be lessons for us in the African experience.

CHAPTER TWO

The Economics of Independence

The leaders of independent Africa have asserted almost unanimously that the political advantage gained through the struggle for independence will be rendered meaningless without a corresponding advance in economic independence and a rise in the standard of living of the mass of the people. The present-day political leadership is fully aware that its future depends on its ability to produce concrete improvements in daily life. Coupled with the political imperative at home for economic improvement is an equally pressing desire to demonstrate political independence on the world scene through achievement of a substantial degree of national economic independence.

Economic decolonization is as important as political decolonization and is much more difficult to achieve. The economies of all the contemporary African states were more or less developed in line with the economic needs of the mother country. They were, and largely still are, producers of primary products which were exported to the European and other external markets in their raw state; in return the colonial economy imported the necessary manufactured goods from the foreign markets. Distribution of these manufactured goods and the purchase of the colonies' raw products were frequently in the hands of large European companies whose agents formed the basis of the wholesale and even retail distribution of consumer goods within the colony.

While the purchasing and the distributing networks set up by these companies provided the bases for a great deal of the African internal trade, they left relatively little scope for the indigenous entrepreneur except at the lowest levels of business. It was only natural, therefore, that one of the first demands of the people and of the new nationalist parties at independence was for a substantially greater share of the operation of business to be placed in local hands. Two major difficulties stood in the way of such a transfer: the lack of trained personnel, particularly at the middle levels of management, who could be expected to take over the functions of commercial middlemen that had been the province of European managers of the trading companies' branches; and the absence of local sources of capital from which indigenous enterprises might be launched. The larger European companies attempted to meet the first difficulty through training programs for local African management, but these were begun too late and often without much enthusiasm. The accumulation of local savings is a rather longer process and may have to be supplemented by the contribution of government capital in the form of loans for the establishment of small business. As these businesses become established it may be expected that the operations of the European trading firms will be more and more withdrawn from the retail level except in the larger centers of trade. Where African governments have sought, as in Guinea, to substitute their own agencies for the private distributors, the results have been generally most unsatisfactory.

The trend over the years since independence has increasingly been toward confining the area of operation of foreign business firms. Partly as a result of governmental financial assistance and partly in consonance with theories of economic development which lay heavy stress on African participation, the role of the indigenous entrepreneur in business has greatly increased, particularly in such countries as Ghana. Government training schemes aimed at Africanization of the economy and pressure upon the foreign firms

to vacate fields of enterprise for which **Africans are** quali-
fied has tended to reduce substantially the role of the for-
eigner in the day-to-day economic transactions of the
country. Since all African governments have engaged to
some degree in long-range economic planning, the foreign
firms are being increasingly forced to adjust their policies
to the goals of these plans.

Quite apart from the conviction of many of the leaders
of the necessity of governmental control over those sections
of the economy which provide key products of mass con-
sumption, it is quite natural that the burden of developing
the economies of the new African states should fall upon
governments. Except for specific products, such as tin in
Nigeria, for which there was a substantial world demand,
the colonial administrations did not see their task primarily
as one of economic development. The job of the colonial
service officer was to *administer,* to maintain law and order
and to produce sufficient resources from the colony to take
care of local budgetary needs. Large-scale economic development was not his province, nor did he have the technical
skills to initiate it. Developmental economics as an applied
skill is essentially a phenomenon of the post-World War II
period, and its application to the independent areas of Africa
requires the services of technically trained personnel, who
would not have been found in the colonial services even if
continued control by the mother country had been possible.

The new governments, then, were the only agencies
that were capable of supplying the capital and hiring the
technical personnel necessary to provide developmental
plans and projects. For the most part the type of development most necessary was that at the level of the infrastructure — roads, bridges, schools, power plants and other public
utilities — which was neither of interest nor of profit to
private capital.

Progress in the creation of an economic infrastructure
is, of course, not only a prerequisite to advances in the
agricultural sector of the African economies, but is of even

greater importance in the process of industrialization to which every African government is committed. While experience thus far has begun to demonstrate that industrialization is not the panacea which some African leaders expected it to be, nevertheless it is clearly necessary in some measure if the African states are to reduce their dependence upon imported manufactured goods — a dependence which is growing constantly greater with the increasing popular demand for luxury goods which are the appurtenances of the successful modernization of the economy. In addition to providing for new requirements in consumer products, industrialization is also needed to give diversification to the local economy. In this way it is hoped to reduce substantially the economic dislocations arising from the price fluctuations on the world market of the primary products which make up a large share of African exports.

Large-scale industrialization requires, however, not only capital but planning, both as regards markets and future manpower requirements. The growing capital needs of the new economies can be met in part from loans or grants made to the new governments, but most governments count also on the additional support of private investment from external sources. Although such investments are needed, they raise the spectre of continued economic domination of the new state from the outside. Nkrumah and other leaders have seen in the creation in Africa of a number of small, relatively weak states an attempt on the part of the colonial powers to replace their former political control by a more subtle form of economic control based on investment. Nkrumah has agreed that the best defense by the African states against this "balkanization" is the retention of a dominating share by the government in enterprises involving foreign capital, and intra-African cooperation, which will strengthen the individual African governments in their resistance to external threats.

However, the continuing supply of capital is only one aspect of industrialization, and the African states are only today becoming aware of the need to coordinate the economic planning for new industries with educational planning in order to make available not only the technicians but the management skills necessary for the establishment of industrial operations. In the face of an oversupply of unskilled primary-school graduates demanding jobs, governments will be required to engage in supplementary training programs to prepare these young people for industry, and in addition the private companies, particularly those under foreign control, will be under great pressure from governments to provide on-the-job training to those who have a minimum of schooling.

Obviously, planned industrial expansion is made much easier if the government can count on the total support of the people, organized by means of the apparatus of the nationalist party. Control over the society, exerted through local party units, permits the government to explain its plans fully to the masses and thus arouse popular enthusiasm for its goals and provide control mechanisms through which the energies and talents of groups within the population can be channeled into those modernizing projects to which the government attaches highest priority. The high degree of organization and discipline achieved through the one-party system assists in promoting the political stability without which the best-laid economic developmental plans cannot hope to achieve their fullest impact on the country. Even the most carefully designed economic plan is more or less susceptible to disruption from purely political considerations which must be taken into account by the ministers and other officials concerned with the implementation of the plans. Economic decisions which may well be theoretically and practically in the best interests of the people as a whole may be nullified if their execution involves the loss of local political support.

It has been argued in Africa that the effectiveness of economic planning is increased in direct proportion to the degree to which party control minimizes the possibility of interference by extraneous political factors. As the example of Guinea has recently indicated, however, it does not follow that the high degree of political stability achieved by a party such as the Parti Démocratique de Guinée guarantees that economic planning will be successful if the planners lack the technical skills needed to carry it out. In attempting to nationalize every sector of the economy as fully as possible, the Guinean party moved too rapidly and without sufficient experience to substitute state control for private operations in all aspects of commerce. This disrupted normal market activity within the country to the point where the continued operation of the economy was seriously threatened. Government ministries possessed neither the personnel nor the technical skill necessary to regulate internal production and distribution, so that private incentive was lost and both imports and exports declined strikingly. By mid-1963, however, the government had recognized its error, and steps were being taken to return the bulk of economic activity in the country to private hands. The Guinean example should not be interpreted to mean that there does not exist in the foreseeable future a substantial role for government in economic development in the new African states. Rather, it is indicative of the fact that governments will begin to find the limits of their abilities to direct economic development, and a compromise position based on the solid foundations of experience will gradually be found between the governmental and the private sectors.

Whatever may be the economic policies of the African governments, inevitably limitations to development are created by the lack of widespread technological knowledge and also by the lack of resources or their maldistribution. While it is true that the continent of Africa contains some of the world's most extensive and varied mineral resources, the basis of the African economy will continue to be in agriculture for the foreseeable future. By far the largest percentage of the African population depends on the working of the soil for its daily existence. With the exception of a few areas, such as the East African highlands, the soils of Africa are not rich. Traditional African farming methods, which permitted natural refertilization by allowing the fields to lie fallow for some period of time, were satisfactory for subsistence farming in areas of relatively light population density, but with the increasing population resulting from modern medical advances, more concentrated farming resulting in greater pressure on the soil is rapidly becoming more common.

The major developmental task, then, of the new African governments must be an agricultural revolution. Industrialization programs may provide a temporary palliative through a reduction of pressure on the land, but in the last analysis even these can only be successful if they go hand in hand with rural improvement programs designed to provide higher living standards for the mass of the peasants. Without this, the new consumer-goods industries will lack the mass market for their products, upon which their expansion depends. But modernization of the agricultural sector of the economy is perhaps everywhere the most difficult task of all, since it depends as much on a slow process of education as on the availability of capital. New techniques of farming must be taught at the same time as the government makes available the tools and fertilizers which these techniques require. Incentives must be evident to persuade the peasant to change his age-old farming methods. Much is being done in many parts of Africa to bring about agricultural change through the use of cooperatives, which provide collectively materials which the individual farmer could not hope to afford. Through them, too, the knowledge of the new skills is being disseminated.

During the period of colonial rule, agricultural development tended to receive rather less than its full share of attention by the administration. Agricultural assistance was concentrated on large projects which would develop agricultural products for export rather than on improving the subsistence crops of the peasant. In part this could be blamed on the limited technical facilities available to the administrations. But also the unorganized mass of the peasantry was unable to make its voice heard effectively to demand its share of the available resources for development. In the areas of European agricultural settlement where the best land and therefore the best basis for increased agricultural production lay, the administrations spent a disproportionate share of the revenues on amenities such as good roads, telephonic communication and electrical services, which were of direct benefit only to the tiny European minority of the population. While it could be argued that the amount spent on paved roads, for example, was of indirect benefit to the African, the fact remains that an equal amount expended on the creation of dirt roads in rural areas where none had existed before would have been of greater assistance to a much larger part of the population. With the coming of independence this trend has not always been reversed; the new governments tend to pay a good deal of lip service to the notion of rural development, but all too often the amount of tax revenues spent on improvement of the urban areas is much greater than can be justified. Urban dwellers are able to put more direct pressures on the government; moreover, one of the most visible signs of independence is the erection of new and splendid government buildings in the capital and other large cities. While these symbols may be of value in establishing national prestige, the rural peasantry gains little from them.

Apart from agriculture, the African continent's greatest wealth lies in its mineral reserves. Some areas, such as Katanga in the Congo Republic and the Copper Belt in Northern Rhodesia, are today reaching an advanced stage of development. It is estimated that the capital invested in the entire mining complex of the copper areas of Northern Rhodesia is in excess of one billion dollars. Similarly, in Liberia, Guinea and Ghana the exploitation of bauxite and iron is being pushed rapidly with capital from European and American sources. However, Africa's mineral wealth is not widespread; it is confined, according to our present geological knowledge, to certain areas and countries. Moreover, regardless of the long-range value of Africa's minerals, in the short run they are of comparatively little value for immediate development purposes. Governments can only realize revenues from them in the form of taxes and royalties if they are exploited. The working of mineral deposits depends on factors outside the control of the African governments. World markets may be oversupplied with certain minerals, making African deposits of little interest to investors. The costs of developing African mineral deposits are frequently abnormally high because they involve not only the mining operation itself but the installation of railroads, port facilities and refining operations which most of the African countries do not as yet possess. Even if there are prospects of overcoming these disadvantages, foreign investors are frequently hesitant to engage in heavy commitments because of doubts of the future political stability of the countries concerned. Africa's mineral wealth will undoubtedly play an important role in the long-range modernization of the continent, but the presence of mineral resources is not to be confused with their short-range value as aids in reaching the pressing economic goals of the new governments.

Despite the difficulties, both physical and psychological, which beset the new African governments in their drive for economic independence, the prospect for a higher standard of living for the mass of Africans is by no means poor. Many African states have made astonishing progress since independence in reorienting their economies away from the more negative aspects of the colonial economic relationship. Whatever may be the pattern of economic organization toward which they are ultimately heading, the new African leaders have shown themselves to be above all realists. They are perfectly well aware that their countries will continue to be dependent on outside technical assistance and investment for a long time. They are prepared to accept this assistance from any source, provided it does not seriously compromise their independence and freedom of action. They realize that all economic aid implies some commitment on their part; the problem is to balance their needs against the possibility of a permanent political tie to any non-African power. In part, at least, the drive for unity which has become so strong a theme in intra-African politics since 1960 is attributable to the desire to find through interdependence within Africa a counterweight to continued dependency on European markets.

The African states are still bound to the former colonial powers by established patterns of trade which will be difficult to break. They are bound, too, by membership in the European currency blocs, the franc zone and the sterling bloc. While many nationalists would like to sever this as well as other visible signs of the former colonial relationship, they are deterred by the serious consequences that may come from freeing their currencies. The only one of the former colonies to create its own currency has been Guinea, and the experience has been far from satisfactory. Guinean francs cannot be exported nor are they accepted outside Guinea. The result has been to cripple trade and to create an internal black market for non-Guinean currencies which the Government has been forced to repress. Mali, on the other hand, has renewed her currency agreement with France so that the Mali franc continues to be backed by the metropolitan franc in the same manner as is the franc of the African Financial Community in the other former French areas.

Most African states continue to receive direct or indirect aid from the metropolitan power. Some of the less well developed French-speaking states receive direct subsidy from the French treasury to balance current operating budgets as well as for capital expenditure. The former British colonies benefit from a variety of development assistance grants, and technical personnel are provided on a contract basis.

The African governments have not tried to conceal their preference for aid from international organizations rather than from Europe, the Eastern bloc or the United States. Such aid, they believe, will have fewer political strings attached to it and, if it comes from agencies of the United Nations, they will have some voice, as U.N. members, in its allocation and use. In addition to the work of the United Nations Special Fund, substantial aid has been given to Africa by the three members of the World Bank group, the Bank itself, the International Development Association and the International Finance Corporation. Loans from these three had totaled over $1 billion by mid-1963, spread over twenty African countries. By far the largest portion ($515 million) of these loans went to the development of internal transportation facilities, particularly for railway extensions. Another substantial share was devoted to the construction of hydroelectric projects such as the Kariba Dam on the Zambezi River between Northern and Southern Rhodesia. Over $70 million was given for direct agricultural assistance and $120 million for industrial projects.

But it is clear that international aid can never be sufficient to satisfy the needs of the African countries. Inevitably they must rely on the help of the two great power blocs, each of which seeks to satisfy its own special interests in extending aid to Africa. American aid is, at least in part, designed to fortify the developing nations against the inroads of Communism, while Soviet aid is yet another weapon in the constant effort to spread Russian influence in Africa. The United States is concerned in its aid programs with the eventual creation of liberal free enterprise economies, capable of satisfying through private industry the basic demands for consumer goods. The Soviets, on the other hand, tend to extend aid for the building up of heavy industry under state control which will begin to provide the base for the growth of an industrial proletariat now lacking in Africa.

American aid to Africa has amounted to more than ten times that of the Soviets, but it has not always been effective in African eyes. The mechanisms for the administration of American aid are too complex, and, because of the limitations of the annual Congressional vote, American help cannot be fully counted upon in the long-term economic planning of the African governments. Soviet aid is much easier to obtain and is frequently granted on more favorable terms. But the African leaders are aware that with it come the psychological pressures of Soviet propaganda media and even the possibility of interference in their internal affairs as the case of the expulsion of the Soviet ambassador from Guinea in 1961 illustrates.

Faced with a continuing critical need for outside technical aid and capital, the African states are forced to turn to the two contending blocs. Both donors claim that the economic system they espouse will open the doors to a better life for the mass of Africans. Meanwhile the African leaders try to maintain political and ideological neutrality while they construct the African road to a modern economic paradise.

CHAPTER THREE

The European in Independent Africa

The nationalism that swept Africa over the past decade found its greatest points of resistance in those areas where there was a substantial European settler population. In the Republic of South Africa there are three Africans to one European. But in the other territories of Africa where there was sizable European settlement — Algeria, Kenya, the former Central African Federation and the overseas provinces of Portugal, Angola and Mozambique — Europeans constitute only a small fraction of the total population. In Algeria, one out of every ten in the population before independence was European; in Kenya, one out of every hundred. In the Central African Federation there were somewhat over 300,000 Europeans to eight million Africans, while in Angola the ratio was one to fifty and in Mozambique less than one to one hundred. However, the smallness of their numbers bore no relation to the political and economic power wielded by the Europeans. In their hands lay the reins of government: for the most part, it was the European minority who chose the members of the legislatures and made up the executives of the civil service. In its hands, too, lay the economic power of the country; Europeans controlled the capital for development and much of the import-export trade, and were, in most cases, the producers of the major export crops.

In the European community, too, were concentrated

the political and technical skills, the result of an educational system which devoted proportionally more of the public funds to European education than to the education of Africans.

In the face of growing African nationalism elsewhere on the continent, the European minorities in these parts of Africa found themselves increasingly under pressure to surrender their positions of power and prestige to the African majority and to assume, in effect, an entirely new position, politically and economically — a position which would at its best be difficult to work out and which at its worst would involve the kind of violence which occurred in Algeria over the seven years of the independence struggle and which still remains a possibility in the southern part of the African continent.

In no area of Africa has a fully successful multi-racial community been worked out as an operating concern. The best hope for a long-range peaceful transition from a government controlled by Europeans to one controlled entirely by Africans in which Europeans will have only minimal political power appears to be in Kenya. The term "multi-racial" is in itself incorrect in this context. The goal toward which Africans and liberal Europeans in the areas of European settlement are striving is not a *multi-racial* state but a *non-racial* state; that is, a state in which the fact of race will not be significant. Multi-racial implies that a distinction is still made as to race but that a compromise solution has been arrived at under which the races can live together in peace. Non-racial, on the other hand, implies that a political structure has been created without regard to race, that an African or a European can be elected to parliament by either African or European voters and that his election will be based only on the criterion of his value as a representative, not on his value as a representative of his particular race.

The dilemma of the multi-racial territories is that, on the one hand, control over the government lies in the hands of the European minority, as in the former Central African Federation and South Africa, while, on the other, the vast majority of the population, the Africans, have little or no say in political decision-making. Only in 1960 did there begin to be an African majority in the government of Kenya; political control was wrested from the European minority in Algeria only at the cost of thousands of lives.

The European minority has often argued that the maintenance of European political control is needed in order to maintain "European standards." This was merely another way of saying that it was necessary to preserve the position of privilege which the Europeans had acquired, for only in this way could the requisite standards be maintained. These "standards" were frequently enshrined in constitutional documents, which, although they may not have mentioned race as a distinctive feature, nevertheless set as the norms of conduct European norms, which, because the Africans could hope to aspire to them only rarely, meant that government would remain, for the foreseeable future at least, in "responsible" European hands. Frequently also the case for European standards was couched in terms of the national interest. It was argued that, were the government to fall into irresponsible (that is, African) hands, foreign investors would be scared off by the political instability that would ensue and that the internal economy of the territory would disintegrate because of the inability of Africans to operate government services and other technical aspects of the economy.

These dire predictions of the European community were often an attempt to camouflage self-interest and to protect its rights by camouflaging them with a professed interest in the nation as a whole. It was, of course, quite easy to prove that Africans were incapable of running the economy because they were as yet insufficiently educated to be able to take over the highly skilled posts of government. But these were self-fulfilling predictions so long as the European community effectively prevented the African from acquiring that education and those technical skills which would, in fact, put the African on a par with the European and thus allow him an equal chance with the European for these governmental posts. The maintenance of "European standards" implied, almost by definition, domination by the European community for the foreseeable future and retention of the majority of technical and skilled posts in European hands. To do this in the face of rising African nationalism meant also that the European community had to keep control of the army and of the police to permit continued control over the African population.

Increasingly, the Europeans felt that they had to isolate themselves from the African lest the African use force to impress his claim upon the white man. In this situation increasing tension could not fail to develop between the two racial communities, as the situation in Northern and Southern Rhodesia has only too clearly demonstrated over the past five years.

The simple fact is that African advance is incompatible with the maintenance of "European standards." Only when, as in Kenya today, the European population can be reconciled to the loss of what are presumed to be "European standards" is there any hope of creating a viable political system which will permit political and constitutional advance by a vote of the African majority.

In South Africa today exactly the reverse course is being pursued. There the maintenance of "European standards" requires, in the eyes of a large section of the European community, the rigid exclusion of the African from any part in political decision-making. The theory of *apartheid*, or separateness, as it has been set forth by the government of Dr. Verwoerd, the Prime Minister, requires the total isolation of one community from the other, not only on the political but on the social and economic levels as well. *Apartheid* envisages the creation of separate political units called Bantustans, which would in effect be new countries for the African population; within these countries African governments would rule more or less along traditional African lines. The argument of the Nationalist Party in South Africa is that this is the only way in which African values and ways of life can be maintained. By separating the two communities entirely, each may maintain its own standards as it sees fit.

Unfortunately, when the theories of *apartheid* are rigidly enforced, as the South African government is attempting to do today, they either break down or they push those who seek to enforce them into ridiculous absurdities. However strongly the outside world may condemn *apartheid* on the grounds of morality or ethical conduct, such condemnation will have little effect on those white South Africans who believe that their theories are justified by their interpretation of the Bible. Much more telling will be the demonstration that these very European standards which *apartheid* seeks to maintain will break down in the face of a total economic divorce of the two communities. European standards in South Africa are themselves dependent on the presence of African labor. The advanced stage of development which the South African economy has reached could not be sustained for long without the employment of Africans in mines and industries. The African, in turn, depends on the European community for his employment. The attempt to destroy the mutual dependence of the two racial communities by the total separation that is *apartheid* can only lead to a reduction in South Africa's economic strength and to bitterness and desperation within the African community, which may end in violence.

The Central African Federation, which was composed of Southern and Northern Rhodesia and Nyasaland, provided from 1953 to 1963 an excellent illustration of the difficulty of working out a satisfactory solution to the problems of government in a multi-racial society. The problems of the Federation were complicated by the differing juridical status of the three territories which were brought together to form the Federation. Northern Rhodesia and Nyasaland were colonies under the jurisdiction of the British Colonial Office, while Southern Rhodesia was termed a self-governing colony, over which the Colonial Office had no direct control. Southern Rhodesia, an area of 150,000 square miles, has a temperate climate and the kind of soil suitable for European agricultural crops. The Europeans living in Southern Rhodesia were chiefly engaged in farming or business. Much of the labor for these Southern Rhodesian farms came from Nyasaland, a narrow strip of land down the shore of Lake Nyasa, which has too great an African population to support on its limited agricultural land. Northern Rhodesia, almost 300,000 square miles in area, is also suitable for European agriculture, but its major importance to the economy of the Federation was the Copper Belt, which produces a substantial portion of the free world's copper.

The idea of federating the three territories goes back almost to the beginning of European settlement. From the outset, federation was advocated by the European minority because it was felt that this would be the most effective way to reduce or eliminate British control over the legislation of Southern Rhodesia. Britain retained a power of veto over certain aspects of the legislation in Southern Rhodesia, particularly those laws which might be detrimental to the African interests. The Europeans long felt that in order to retain control over the government in the face of rising African demands for a share of political power, full powers had to be retained within the territory and not shared with London, despite the fact that the British government made virtually no use of the powers which were reserved to it.

During the period between the two wars, two Royal Commissions were appointed by the British government to look into the question of future amalgamation or federation of the three territories. Both reported back that such a step was not desirable, the major reasons advanced being that the native policies of the three territories were incompatible with federation. The policy pursued in Southern Rhodesia of the gradual growth of African participation through partnership differed substantially from the policies of African advance pursued in Northern Rhodesia and Nyasaland, where under the control of the Colonial Office there were, theoretically at least, no barriers to greater African participation in government.

From the outset the Federation was opposed by the Africans, first by the chiefs and later by the leaders of the new African political parties. The African majority quite correctly assumed that federation or amalgamation of the territories would tend to preserve European political control. With the restraints of the British Colonial Office removed, the European minority would be free to impose a rate of development on the African population which could be regulated to preserve European control almost indefinitely.

The major European argument in favor of federation was economic. The physical resources of the three territories were complementary. The labor of Nyasaland was needed on the farms and in the mines of the other two territories, and it was argued that the economic development of the territories for the good of all concerned would be more rapid and more rational if there could be developed common governmental services and transport facilities, and coordinated governmental planning. Federation, it was claimed, would secure the most efficient use of economic resources, raw materials and technical skills. A single government for the federation would be able to attract outside investment more easily, in the view of the European minority, and as a consequence the African majority would progress more rapidly toward a higher standard of living.

There was no doubt that distinct economic advantages were to be derived from coordinated planning of development in the three territories, and a stronger federal government seemed likely to be able to provide a more stable political climate for the attraction of overseas capital. But the African leaders were not prepared to accept the economic advantages of federation, although they essentially agreed with the arguments for them, at the cost of sacrificing any hope of political advancement and eventual control of government by the majority of the people.

Undeterred by the African opposition and the reluctance of the British government to undertake discussions regarding federation, the European leadership continued to press the issue. During the war years it was dropped, but after a series of conferences in 1951 and 1952 between the European political leaders in Southern Rhodesia and the Colonial Office, federation came into being on September 1, 1953. The African leaders boycotted all of these discussions, and the final vote, taken as a referendum in Southern Rhodesia only, since Northern Rhodesia and Nyasaland were under the control of the Colonial Office, in April, 1953, registered 25,000 voters *for* and 14,000 *against* federation. This meant, in effect, that only 39,000 voters, all but 400 of them Europeans, registered their opinion on federation, and even of this 39,000, some one-third voted against it.

The course of development pursued by the Federal government after 1953 rapidly proved that the African fears of the consequences of federation had been well founded. The leader of the majority European political party in Northern and Southern Rhodesia (the United Federal Party), Sir Roy Welensky, made it clear that the Federation was not to mean any deviation from the line of maintaining "European standards." Even in the course of the first election campaign in 1953 for the Federal legislature, it was declared, "The Federal Party is determined to see that there will be no lowering of European standards," which meant, in effect, that Africans had to exert themselves if they wished to rise to a higher level. In the political field the African could enjoy only such share of political control as he was capable of earning by demonstrating that he had attained "civilized" or "European" standards of behavior and culture.

The basic policy upon which the multi-racial community was to be developed was that of partnership, which implied, in effect, a constitutional arrangement by which the

Europeans and Africans would act as partners in the development of the Federation. The only difficulty, of course, was that the Africans were to be very junior partners. The relationship was somewhat unfortunately described by a prominent European as that between the horse and the rider; the African majority needed no explanation as to which was which.

However good the intentions of the leadership of the Federation may have been in 1953 to implement partnership and racial equality, the years following proved to Africans that partnership was increasingly a hollow myth. Under the growing pressure of African political demands, a number of minor concessions were made, but in Southern Rhodesia the Europeans remained in complete control. Political advance for the Southern Rhodesian African has been desperately slow, although in all three territories African political parties have come into existence. In Northern Rhodesia the dominant African party, the United National Independence Party (UNIP) under the leadership of Kenneth Kaunda, secured adherents throughout the colony, pressed for an African majority in the legislature, and secured the promise from the British Government of independence in 1964. In Nyasaland, Dr. Hastings Banda's Malawi Congress Party took over the reins of power in 1960, with the prospect of full independence also in 1964. In Southern Rhodesia, on the contrary, the European Government added to African frustration by repeatedly banning the Nationalist Party led by Joshua Nkomo, only to have it reappear under another name within a few months.

The rate of growth of African political consciousness was far ahead of that of partnership and the African rejection of federation became more and more bitter. A Federal election was called by Prime Minister Sir Roy Welensky, in April of 1962, chiefly on the issue of the maintenance of the Federation. Sir Roy's party, which had the support of the majority of Europeans in Northern and Southern Rhodesia, was returned to power, but in the actual circumstances his victory was virtually meaningless, since those **Africans** who were allowed to vote boycotted the elections. Therefore, the vast majority of Africans had no say, and desired no say, in the maintenance of federation. For them the equality of economic, social and political opportunity promised by partnership was still very far in the future. For the most part, Africans depended on the land for their livelihood, and the Land Apportionment Act in Southern Rhodesia reserved the best of the agricultural land for the Europeans only. While European migration into Southern Rhodesia did increase during the past decade, the African population and therefore the African pressure on the land grew even more rapidly.

By 1962 African pressure to destroy the Central African Federation had become so strong that the British government could no longer support the demand of the Southern Rhodesian Europeans for preservation of the *status quo*. The creation of an African majority in the Northern Rhodesian Legislative Council was the signal for the beginning of the breakup; it became even clearer with the acknowledgment by Britain of the right of the component parts of the Federation to secede. Both Kaunda and Banda announced their intention of taking their countries out of the Federation, and, despite the most strenuous efforts of Sir Roy Welensky, the ill-fated Federation disappeared on December 31, 1963.

For the Europeans of Southern Rhodesia the time was rapidly passing, if it had not already done so, when their position could be maintained without violence and use of force against the growing strength of African nationalism. Were such a clash to take place, the result would seem inevitable in the long run, for even if the organized force of the Europeans were able to preserve control for a period of time, the corrosive effects of internal dissent would eventually be ruinous to the economy.

The situation prevailing in Angola and Mozambique seems much less amenable to settlement without violence than does that in Southern Rhodesia. Portugal regards these two African territories as overseas provinces, constitutionally and administratively an extension and integral part of the homeland. For this reason, the Portuguese government has refused to consider the question of independence, or even to admit the right of African nationalists to press for it.

The Portuguese position rests on a strong sense of the past. For over four hundred years the Portuguese were engaged in their "civilizing mission" not only in Africa but in Asia and Latin America, and the Portuguese empire was once one of the greatest in the world. The Portuguese are determined to pursue, in the few possessions remaining to them, their historic mission, which they see as making the African "savage" into a reasonable facsimile of the "civilized" Western man. The Portuguese have traditionally pursued a policy of assimilation whereby an African who received an education to the point where he accepted the life of the European could be accepted legally and socially as a Portuguese citizen. In an attempt to decrease the pressures of African nationalism, recent legislation has made all Africans of the overseas provinces citizens of the motherland regardless of their educational level.

But this gesture will do little to make up for the years of exploitation of the African which Portuguese colonial policy produced. The *regime do indigenato* under which the vast majority of Africans lived gave the Portuguese administrator almost total control over the lives of the Africans under his jurisdiction. In theory and in legislation which was observed more in the breach than in practice, the African was protected against the labor demands of the Portuguese planter, but he was also expected, as part of the civilizing process, to learn the value of work. Not infrequently this lesson was impressed on him through forced labor on the farms of the Europeans.

Portuguese authorities have insisted that the foreign press has given a false picture of Portuguese rule in Angola and Mozambique. Instead of resisting assimilation, they argue, the African has come to appreciate the social and economic progress which it allows. African children are taught Portuguese in bush schools and are then permitted to advance toward further primary and secondary education. Once they have embarked on this path they are treated in exactly the same way as the children of Portuguese parents. Again, the theory is true, but, partly because of the financial limitations of the Portuguese administration, only a tiny fraction of the African children can take advantage of the system.

But it is not so much the abuses of the system that the African nationalists object to; they are aware that Portugal's resources are limited, even if they feel that much more could be done than is at present. Rather it is the basic refusal of the Portuguese to entertain the notion of the African right to self-determination that has caused Holden Roberto, the Angolan nationalist leader, to establish a government-in-exile at Leopoldville which is recognized by many of the African states. Roberto's forces opened a guerrilla campaign against well-armed and trained Portuguese troops, and by the end of 1963 the rebels controlled portions of northern Angola. A similar but less fully organized group whose goal is independence for Mozambique has sprung up at Dar-es-Salaam.

The Portuguese administration has sought to dismiss the growing evidence of African nationalism as merely the work of malcontents or Communist agitators. But in the face of the combined pressures of the independent states to the north, there does not appear to be much hope that the Portuguese government can remain indifferent to nationalist demands. Because of the superior arms of the Portuguese troops, the nationalists cannot mount a head-on assault. They hope, however, slowly to erode Portuguese strength by widening the front of their guerrilla attack and by creating sufficient economic dislocation to offset the administration's efforts to build up the boom created by increased settlement from the mother country over the past decade. As in Southern Rhodesia, however, European economic and military control will not be easily broken. The Portuguese provinces may well be among the last strongholds of colonialism in Africa.

Kenya became an independent state in December, 1963, without strong objection from the European minority. This territory had, of course, had its period of serious disturbances during the Mau Mau uprising at the beginning of the last decade. In many ways the Mau Mau uprising, for all its grimness, had a great deal to do with reconciling the Kenya settlers to the possibility of an African-controlled government. It became clear that unless concessions were made to the African majority permitting their leaders to share in the decisions of government, life for the European in Kenya would become intolerable.

On the African side it should be added that Mau Mau brought a new sense of political responsibility to the African leaders. When they were allowed to organize political parties after the end of the emergency they pressed for full African participation in government on a basis of "one man, one vote" but were careful at the same time to reassure the European settler community of a continuing role in Kenyan life. After the election of 1960 the transition was made to an African-controlled government which led the country to independence. It is perhaps symbolic of the power of African nationalism that the leader of Kenya's first independent African government was Jomo Kenyatta, who had been condemned by the British Governor in 1960 as "an implacable opponent of any cooperation with other people, tribes or races who live in Kenya."[1] In the face of the evidently overwhelming demand by the African majority to assume its rightful role as the master of its own house, the European minority, however reluctantly, surrendered its power. It remains to be seen how well the Europeans can learn to live in a country where they were once the rulers and where

[1]Cited in George Delft, *Jomo Kenyatta: Towards Truth About "The Light of Kenya;"* New York, Doubleday & Co., 1961, p. 205.

now their role is virtually that of an economic interest group — albeit a most powerful one — in the framework of an African society.

For the Europeans of South and Central Africa the same lesson will have to be learned. But for them time is running out. The real question is whether they can accept the fact of African control before the patience of the mass of Africans is exhausted.

CHAPTER FOUR

The Drive toward African Unity

A major focus of the relations between African states as they have gradually become independent since 1958 has been the attempt to find some basis for unification. Without exception, the leadership of the new states has placed African unity in the forefront of the goals of foreign policy for their countries. On the surface it may seem somewhat paradoxical that these new states, having gone through the bitter struggle for self-identification and the attainment of sovereignty, should be so eager to surrender a part or even all of their newfound sovereignty to a larger body in which they would be but constituent units. Not all have been in favor of the kind of total unification and submergence within the federal structure that has been the theme of the leader of Ghana, Kwame Nkrumah. But all have been prepared to make at least some sacrifice of their complete independence in order to gain a greater measure of African unity and cooperation.

The commitment of the African leaders to unification stems from the feeling that only in this way can the ultimate objectives of the African revolution be accomplished. Although successful political action had brought independence to most of Africa by 1963, the African revolution in the eyes of today's leaders will not be finished until all of Africa is free and united. Full political equality for Africans in the eyes of the outside world will only come, it is argued, when

Africa speaks with a united voice, although, it should be added, there is little inclination to sacrifice for unity the individual vote in the United Nations of each new state.

Reinforcing the political argument for unification is the cultural claim expressed in such terms as *négritude* and "African personality." *Négritude,* a term most closely associated with the writings of Léopold Senghor, the President of Senegal, has been defined, albeit of necessity vaguely, as a *Weltanschauung,* an expression of the innate emotional qualities which bind Negroes of the world together. One recent commentator insists that *négritude* is not

> ... a preconceived doctrine, elaborated from *a priori* concepts. It claims to rest upon Negro-African realities from which it draws its substance and its being. It tries to translate on the basis of systematic philosophy the values of Negro-African civilization.... The theory of négritude must be placed in the historical, economic and social context of the African world. The Negro is not radically different from the white man or the yellow man solely by the fact that he is black. It is the milieu in which he lives that conditions his reactions, that fashions his mind and his feelings: in a word, which gives a particular tone and expression to every manifestation of his being.[1]

Some African writers see *négritude* as the African response to such foreign ideologies as Communism because it seeks to identify true Negro-African values; in itself it becomes a defense by the Negro-African world against Communism. "It is," says Doudou Thiam, "for the black world what pan-Arabism is for the Arab world."

The expression "African personality," on the other hand, tends to have a much more geographically confined content and specifically political significance than has *négritude.* As used by Kwame Nkrumah, it refers to those traits of character or personality which are specifically African and which imply an African way of political, social or economic organization which is distinct from that to be found elsewhere in the world. The psychological basis, then, of African unity derives from those aspects of personality which are common to all Africans. Closely related to this is

---

[1] Doudou Thiam, *La Politique étrangère des états africains* (Paris, 1963), pp. 20-21.

the theme of an earlier unity of parts of Africa such as the old empires of the Sahara, the Ashanti federation and the Yoruba kingdoms, which are cited as proof that there exists a historical basis for African regional unity predating European contact which can be revived as the basis for a larger contemporary union.

However strong may be the sentimental arguments for African unity, they are overshadowed by self-evident practical arguments in the economic and administrative realms. There is no doubt that long-range economic development in Africa would be facilitated by elimination of tariff barriers (even though intra-African trade is not yet of major importance), the rationalization of economic planning for larger areas (which would be a step toward the creation of larger internal markets), and the cooperative exploitation and use of economic resources. From an administrative point of view, the breakup of the extended geographical units which existed under the colonial administrations, such as the former federations of French West Africa and French Equatorial Africa, has been a serious disadvantage to the new African states. Technical services such as public health and communications which previously existed on a common basis must now be provided individually by each government. In many cases, the lack of trained personnel combined with the additional cost of providing an individual rather than a joint service has meant that even where they have been continued, the quality of former services has not been maintained. Although the differing colonial administrative structures might make it more difficult to establish joint services for the former British and French territories, re-establishment of these services for the large areas of Africa formerly under French administration would not only result in a budgetary saving but would maintain and strengthen the bonds which were previously established on a non-political level between the now independent units of former French Africa.

The arguments for greater unity in Africa, then, are

valid on many other levels than the purely political. But it is the political arguments which have posed the greatest problems in promoting unification and have created endless debate over the methods by which unification should be brought about and over the constitutional form under which a united Africa might come into being.

In this discussion two major themes have predominated. One, whose major spokesman is Kwame Nkrumah of Ghana, emphasizes immediate political unification with a subsequent growth of economic cooperation. It is this approach which is most strictly identified with "Pan-Africanism," although the term has been loosely used in connection with both themes. The other, stemming more directly from Houphouet-Boigny of the Ivory Coast, Tafawa Balewa of Nigeria, and other leaders of the Monrovia group of states, stresses the priority of gradual economic cooperation from which may evolve, at some later and unspecified date, a loose political confederation whose structure is still not clear. The two themes were finally brought together in May, 1963, at the Addis Ababa Conference, from which emerged the Organization of African Unity, which is to constitute the formal base upon which a wider African unity is henceforth to be developed.

Immediate Political Unification

Pan-Africanist doctrine had its origins outside the continent of Africa. In its early years, it was most closely associated with the name of the late Dr. W.E.B. Dubois, whose personality was so strongly impressed upon a series of pan-Africanist conferences held in London and Paris prior to World War II. The early conception of the pan-Africanist movement under Dubois was that of a world organization of Negroes, designed to form a united front in the battle to gain equality for the Negro people. Only after 1945 did pan-Africanism move to Africa where African nationalism replaced the theme of Negro nationalism of the pre-World War II period. George Padmore, the West Indian theorist of pan-Africanism, expressed the new direction of the movement in these terms:

> Pan-Africanism looks above the narrow confines of race, class, tribe and religion. Its vision stretches far beyond the frontiers of the nation state. Its perspective embraces the federation of regional self-governing countries and their ultimate amalgamation into a United States of Africa.

The passionate commitment of Kwame Nkrumah to pan-Africanism can only be appreciated in the light of his early connections with George Padmore, and as co-secretary with Jomo Kenyatta of the Pan-Africanist Conference in Manchester, England, in 1945.

Nkrumah placed pan-Africanism at the cornerstone of the foreign policy of an independent Ghana, and almost since the day of Ghana's independence he has proclaimed the necessity of building a United States of Africa designed to band together the independent states of the continent into a single political federation which would, in some aspects at least, resemble the constitutional structure of the United States of America. Carrying out the promises made at the Manchester Conference, President Nkrumah lost no time in making his first move toward the realization of the pan-Africanist ideal. In April, 1958, he called together a meeting of the heads of the independent African states, and in December of the same year, Ghana was host to the first meeting of the All African Peoples Conference which brought to Accra representatives of the political parties in both independent and still-colonial Africa. By a resolution approved at the Conference, the principle of pan-Africanism was enthusiastically endorsed.

The first concrete steps toward African political unification came with the creation shortly afterward, on December 23, 1958, of the Ghana-Guinea union, to which Mali was added in 1960. It was hoped that this would form a nucleus of a federal union for the United States of Africa, and that other nations would adhere voluntarily to this union. The terms of the union included a common legislature, juridical institutions, currency and flag, and coordinated economic policies. However, the ambitious plans for the union never came to full fruition, since it was beset from the outset by practical problems which were never overcome. The geographic separation of the founding units and the fundamental differences in the institutional structures, administrations and juridical systems of the two governments, added to the differences in language, made any steps toward achieving a set of common institutions very hard to realize. Apart from a loan of ten million pounds from Ghana to its new partner, Guinea, at the outset, and mutual representation of the two countries at the cabinet level, little of a lasting nature came from this first experiment.

Another and, in terms of its influence on international politics, more effective attempt to establish pan-Africanist unity was made by this same group at a conference held in January, 1961, at Casablanca, attended by the Ghana-Guinea-Mali powers, as well as Morocco, Libya, the provisional government of Algeria, and the United Arab Republic. The membership of the Casablanca group was initially the result of a combination of common interests which brought together the North African states and a group of states south of the Sahara. The North African states, and Morocco in particular, were concerned with securing support in Africa south of the Sahara against the so-called Brazzaville group of twelve French-speaking states, which had been formed the previous month. Morocco sought, too, the support of the black African states in its conflict with Mauritania. At the same time, President Nkrumah of Ghana was interested in gaining broader intra-African support for his growing objections to the conduct of the United Nations in the Congo conflict. President Nasser, of the United Arab Republic, was anxious to reinforce Egyptian influence in Africa south of the Sahara and to counteract the growing interest of the African states in Israeli economic aid.

The personal interests of the various members of the Casablanca group became evident in the resolutions of the

Conference, which tended to reveal the mutual concessions that each had made to insure the support of the others for his particular point of view. The issue of African unity played an important role in the deliberations at the Casablanca meeting. The Casablanca Charter which was issued at the end of the meeting looked forward to the establishment of a Consultative Assembly of the states of Africa and, through political, economic and cultural committees, encouraged the finding of common solutions to African problems. The Casablanca group condemned colonialism in the strongest terms, sharply emphasizing the dangers of neo-colonialism and balkanization in Africa. It strongly supported African cooperation in aiding the struggle for independence in Algeria.

Gradual Unification

It was perhaps inevitable that the emphasis placed on the priority of political unification in the Ghana-Guinea-Mali union and in the conception of a pan-Africanist political federation implied by the Consultative Assembly projected at Casablanca should have brought forth a reaction. While the majority of African leaders were undoubtedly in favor of the ultimate goal of unity, increasingly the difference in approach became evident between those "revolutionary" pan-Africanists represented by President Nkrumah, who saw political unity as the first step, and the "moderates," who believed that political unification would follow only as a natural consequence of the identification of common economic interests. Initially, the point of view which stressed the gradual approach was represented by the Conseil de l'Entente, composed of the Ivory Coast, Upper Volta, Niger and Dahomey. Following the leadership of the Ivory Coast, the governments of the other three powers worked toward the goal of full economic cooperation but with no concession to political unification.

The mutual bonds of language and colonial administrative structure prompted the French-speaking states of West and Central Africa to join in an exploration of common economic problems and in the formulation of a common policy in foreign affairs. From the deliberations at Brazzaville emerged the Union of African States and Madagascar (UAM), better known as the Brazzaville Twelve. The resolutions agreed upon at the meeting had a pragmatic content which contrasted clearly with the somewhat emotional tone of the statements on pan-Africanism which had emanated from the leaders of the Ghana-Guinea union. The Brazzaville group addressed itself to such practical questions as the development of a common credit policy and common markets and the growth of commercial exchange between members, the harmonization of national development plans and investment codes, and a discussion of the problems of the African states in their relations with the European Common Market. To implement the economic cooperation envisaged by the resolutions, there was established the Organisation Afro-Malagache de Coopération Economique (OAMCE) at a conference in Yaoundé in March, 1961. In his opening speech to the Yaoundé meeting, President Ahidjo of the Cameroon defined the difference between the Brazzaville group and the Casablanca powers in this way:

> We rapidly realized that *a priori* political institutions are merely empty frameworks even though they may be generally more flattering and fuller of resounding phrases and that they ultimately disappear into the shadows if they are not supported by a deeper and more basic reality which gives them strength and consistence. This is why we wanted to begin at the beginning, before turning toward long-term political objectives which in themselves will become more precise with the growth of our technical organization.[2]

Although the Brazzaville group was initially conceived as an organization of the French-speaking states, it rapidly became clear that there were sufficient common economic interests between the members of this group and neighboring English-speaking states to extend the foundations

---

[2] Thiam, *op. cit.*, pp. 74-5.

laid at Brazzaville and Yaoundé to include other states whose leaders believed in the primacy of economic interest as an element in the development of African unity. In May, 1961, a group of twenty states met at Monrovia, ostensibly to discuss the Congolese situation, but in reality to explore the possibilities of wider African cooperation on both the political and economic levels. Although all the independent African states were invited to attend the Conference, the members of the Casablanca group refused. From the Monrovia meeting of the Inter-African and Malagasy States Organization, as the Monrovia group was formally known, there emerged resolutions urging further steps toward economic cooperation in the fields of trade, currency and banking, the details of which were to be worked out by a series of meetings of experts during the following six months. On the political level, the Monrovia powers stressed the importance of the sovereignty of the individual members, condemning the interference of any outside power, whether African or non-African, in the affairs of African states. This did not mean, however, that in their eyes African countries were precluded from assisting nationalist movements elsewhere in non-independent Africa. The conclusions at Monrovia emphasized the already expressed attitude of the states represented there regarding the continued preservation of full political sovereignty within the broader framework of the gradual development of mechanisms for economic cooperation. This was further confirmed at a subsequent meeting of heads of state in Lagos in January, 1962, from which came the Lagos Charter, the Monrovia group's equivalent of the Casablanca Charter. In his opening speech to the Lagos meeting, Dr. Nnamdi Azikiwe, then Governor-General and now President of Nigeria, declared that the basic difference between the Monrovia and Casablanca groups was the absence of a declaration by the latter group recognizing the legal equality of all African powers, regardless of their size, and affirming the necessity to preserve all states from interference in their internal affairs through subversive activities engineered by supposedly friendly states. It was clear that the Monrovia group felt that economic cooperation should be a matter of technical concern with as little of a political overtone as possible.

Despite the seeming conflict between the Casablanca and Monrovia groups on the techniques of achieving unification in Africa, the economic goals of the two groups were essentially similar. Although President Nkrumah's pan-Africanism envisaged creation of the larger political structure first, the concrete results of the Casablanca Charter, and the Charter of Lagos, were accomplished primarily at the technical working-committee level, where it was sought to harmonize the economic interests of the members of the two groups. This tendency toward regional organizations with economic cooperation was illustrated in East Africa as well as in West Africa. The four ex-British colonies of East Africa — Tanganyika, Uganda, Zanzibar and Kenya — had been moving, even before all were independent, toward a limited form of East African federation, which was embodied in the East African Common Services Organization, the basis for which had already been laid under the British colonial administration.

Eventual political federation of East African territories was envisaged by the leaders of the Pan-African Freedom Movement of East Central and Southern Africa (PAFMECSA), which, as its name indicates, looked toward an extension of a purely East African federation which might at some future date encompass the members of the former Central African Federation — Northern and Southern Rhodesia and Nyasaland — as well as the smaller states of Ruanda and Burundi. But, as in West Africa, the problems involved in economic and administrative cooperation among the members of the potential East African Federation are much easier to solve than are those of harmonizing the complex political interests of the sovereign states concerned.

The Organization of African Unity

The members of these regional groupings of states were finally brought together, along with the North African states (which had not been represented at Lagos), in a single organization with the establishment in May, 1963, at Addis Ababa, of the Organization of African Unity. The new organization, which was to include all the states of continental Africa and the islands surrounding the continent, was designed:

> ... to promote the unity and solidarity of the African states; to coordinate and intensify the cooperation and efforts to achieve a better life for the peoples of Africa; to defend their sovereignty; to eradicate all forms of colonialism in Africa; and to promote international cooperation having due regard to the Charter of the United Nations and the Universal Declaration of Human Rights.

However, it was clearly re-emphasized at the Addis Ababa meeting that to secure these ends those states that joined the Organization were to preserve their full independence of action while coordinating their general policies in the political, economic and educational fields and technical cooperation. No mention was made in the Charter of African Unity of Nkrumah's ideas of political federation; the supreme body of the Organization of African Unity is the Assembly of Heads of States and Governments. In this Assembly, each state possesses one vote, and resolutions can be passed only by a vote of two-thirds of the members. At the executive level of the new Organization is the Council of Ministers, which implements the decisions of the Assembly; it, too, is composed of representatives, each of whom has a single vote.

The OAU represents one further step toward the goal of African unification. It was made clear for the first time at Addis Ababa that the African community was to include the states of North Africa as well as those south of the Sahara. Stress was laid on the gradual development of unity through the creation of an ideology which would be based on an African system of values. Yet the OAU underscores the view of African leaders that the foundation of unity will be the sovereign state, which will determine the form and degree of its cooperation entirely on the basis of its own policy decisions. On these foundations will be erected a framework of organized but voluntary cooperation and coordination which will continue to leave room for the regional organizations which have already made their contribution to African solidarity.

It is as yet too soon to evaluate the possible contributions of the OAU to African unification. To implement the offer of assistance by the independent African states to all national liberation movements in colonial Africa, a Committee of Nine, sitting in Dar-es-Salaam, was established to manage the special fund to be contributed by the members of the OAU for assistance to these movements. The work of this Committee will undoubtedly be of value in coordinating the efforts of the various nationalist parties in the remaining colonies, but the limited financial resources of the African states will prevent any large-scale assistance to underground nationalist forces in southern Africa.

A few months after its birth, the new Organization was called upon to mediate a dispute between two of its members, when the Algerian-Moroccan border question was submitted to an OAU-appointed commission. While it cannot be expected that the OAU will in itself be able to enforce, or even necessarily to find, a long-term *modus vivendi* between the two parties, it nevertheless provides a mechanism whereby a "cooling-off period" can be arranged within which the contending parties may be persuaded to come to agreement. The important point is, however, that there now exists an African mechanism for the solution of intra-African disputes to which the states concerned can appeal before going to a non-African agency. Adherence to the Organization of African Unity and the public pronouncements by African leaders in favor of unification will inevitably put a certain amount of pressure on the parties to an African dispute to seek first the assistance of the OAU in settling their difficulties. In the immediate future, then, it may be expected that the functions of the Organization of African Unity will be primarily those of coordination and facilitation of closer harmony between a group of sovereign members, whose commitment to political unity may be no greater now than it was at Monrovia.

The Future of African Unity

From a doctrinal and ideological standpoint, pan-Africanism has played an important role in the immediate pre-independence and post-independence period in developing a sense of solidarity within the new African community. It has been used, particularly by President Nkrumah, as a rallying cry around which to gather the nationalist forces for the common struggle to liberate all of Africa from colonial rule. Pan-Africanism has been used, too, as a means to reinforce the sense of independence gained from the possession of an exclusively African ideological point of view. The sense of common purpose deriving from pan-Africanism provides protection against the threat of neo-colonialism from the West and the new imperialism of the East. During this period immediately after independence, when the African governments are groping for a position of strength both at home and within the broader context of African and international politics, the ideal of pan-African unity gives strength to resist the encroachments of external ideologies from whatever source.

Pan-Africanism has not, however, always meant a positive source of strength. There has existed the uneasy suspicion, particularly on the part of some of the French-speaking African leaders, that the motivations of those who most loudly proclaim the ideals of pan-African unity are not always pure. The question of the leadership of the pan-African federation, and particularly the possible role of President Nkrumah and of Ghana in such a federation, has been one of the major reasons for the constant reiteration at intra-African gatherings of the theme that territorial integrity and national sovereignty must continue to be respected. As the members of the African community grow farther and farther away from the moment of independence, diverse national interests have inevitably developed, which tend to take precedence over the anti-imperialist and anti-Communist aspects of pan-African unity. As the Foreign Minister of Senegal has pointed out:

> Pan-Africanism remains, above everything, a conception without sharply defined boundaries which rests at one and the same time on realities and on myths. The realities are those of the same continent, similar economic and social conditions, the solidarity created by the colonial experience that all the peoples of Africa have experienced and are still experiencing. The myths are a group of ideas, feelings, beliefs, sometimes legends, which, put together, make the pan-African ideal and which cause Africans to believe in a common destiny.
>
> A mixture of realities and myths, pan-Africanism is also a mixture of contradictory elements. It is a supernationalism that claims to embrace all of Africa, or at least all of one part of Africa.... but it is a supernationalism that contains within it the germs of an imperialism. It is a unifying current opposed by centrifugal forces that contain factors of discord and dislocation.[3]

Although there is an element of persuasive mystique about the doctrine of pan-Africanism, there are also formidable roadblocks in the way of realizing any real degree of African unification. Some of these stem from the cultural heritage of Africa, some have been created by the colonial powers, and some are the creations of the new nationalist governments themselves. Differences of language and cultural background, and ancient tribal rivalries, are natural barriers to African solidarity. Despite the desire of the nationalist leaders to overcome the colonial heritage, the most natural groupings of the African states appear to be of those whose colonial background is similar. Not only did the colonial powers establish common administrative systems for their colonies, but their cultural influences upon their colonials were deeper than many Africans themselves realized. Between this generation of the African leadership,

[3]Thiam, *op. cit.*, p. 31.

at least in French-speaking Africa, and France itself, there is frequently a much greater understanding than between Africans of French and British colonial backgrounds. As the Ghana-Guinea union clearly proved, it will be some time before common institutions can be devised for countries which were the product of two different colonial systems. The struggle for independence was carried out by the nationalist parties on a basis of the existing colonial territories, and emphasis since independence has been heavily on the creation of nations within present boundaries. The new governments have sought to create Ghanaians, Nigerians or Senegalese first, and stress upon the common African background has been a distinctly secondary consideration. A common African bond was forged in the anti-colonial struggle which has carried over into the post-independence period, but this is not enough to overcome the growing diversity of national interests. Nor has tribal solidarity proved a unifying factor to the degree that might have been expected; despite the fact that the artificial boundaries carved out by the European powers for their units of colonial control frequently split tribal areas, tribal reunification has only been an element in two border rectifications, one involving the former British trust territory of West Cameroon, which, by United Nations-conducted plebiscite, joined the former French Camerouns to become part of the Cameroon Republic, the other, Somalia. Therefore, the colonial experience has proved ultimately to be a much more unifying influence than that provided by tribal structure.

In view of the repeatedly expressed desire for economic cooperation and the numerous inter-governmental committees and commissions which have been set up to promote mutual economic interests, there has as yet been relatively little evidence of the desire on the part of African states to take concrete steps toward pooling natural resources, nor for the sharing of resources by the richer members of the African community to aid the development of those less well endowed. The new governments see the utilization of resources first as a means of raising the living standards of their own people and not in the light of the common needs of the African community. The opposition of M. Houphouet-Boigny, the president of the Ivory Coast, to perpetuating the former federation of French West Africa was undoubtedly accounted for in part by his disinclination to share the resources of the Ivory Coast with the other members of the federation, while a similar position toward the French Equatorial Federation was taken by the government of Gabon.

The whole blame for the failure so far to share available resource revenues cannot be laid at the door of the new nationalist governments; the lesson had already been taught them by the previous colonial administrations. Scarcely any cooperative effort was made by Britain, France, Belgium and Portugal to engage in common economic planning for their African colonies prior to independence. Each colony was encouraged to develop its own potential with little or no thought given to the plans of the neighboring colonies. Since independence, the competition between the European states, the United States and the Soviet bloc to give aid to the African countries has done little to ameliorate the earlier lack of planning. Thus, costly ports are today being developed all along the West African coast with outside aid so that each country may have a well-equipped port of its own. Yet, correspondingly large amounts of money are not being invested in road and rail transportation to the interior which would facilitate bringing to the coast the very products which the new ports are designed to handle.

The leaders of the African states appear to be paying relatively little heed to President Nkrumah's warnings about the dangers of balkanization and neo-colonialism. Despite their lip-service to the cause of African economic cooperation, many leaders seem more concerned with the future of their relationship to the European market for their primary products than they are with the building up of the intra-

African market. The present state of intra-African trade makes the prospect of an African Common Market very distant, and its advantages at best dubious, so long as many African countries (particularly the former French colonies) can expect to derive substantial trade benefits and financial support in a continuing relationship with the European Common Market. A step toward a tightly knit African economic community has been taken with the establishment of the African Development Bank and the African Economic Institute, but the effects of these institutions will not be immediately evident.

While regional blocs may hold out somewhat better immediate prospects for acceptance as one stage in African unification than does the over-all political federation favored by Dr. Nkrumah, even these regional units, seen as building blocks toward the larger whole, have a very questionable future. The colonial federations have been broken up, and the experiments in federation tried since independence have failed almost uniformly. The Ghana-Guinea union accomplished little, and the Federation of Mali lasted only a short time. The Conseil de l'Entente, while still existing, has shown signs of internal disagreement.

The whole question of regional groupings caused much discussion at Addis Ababa and at the subsequent meeting of the foreign ministers at Dakar. As early as 1958 the All African Peoples Conference had agreed that "the independent states of Africa should amalgamate themselves into groups on the basis of geographical contiguity, economic interdependence and linguistics and cultural affinity." But when states such as the group of twenty PAFMECSA members did just this, they aroused the ire of President Nkrumah, who condemned regional groups for their tendency to disperse energy and resources which might better be used in the greater work of promoting political federation.

Still, at Addis Ababa the trend was strongly toward favoring regional arrangements, since they were at least capable of producing agreement on a limited range of common interests. The later Dakar meeting of foreign ministers discussed the question of the definition of regional groupings, finally resolving that they could be justified only on the basis of "geographical realities and economic and social conditions common to neighboring states." The dissolution of the Ghana-Guinea-Mali union and the Casablanca group were proclaimed, but the members of the UAM were reluctant to dissolve the organization, despite the fact that it did not meet the conditions of the resolution, until the concrete advantages of exclusive participation in the OAU could be clearly weighed against their common interest in continued French treasury subsidies and development aid from the French Economic Community. The UAM members were disposed to wait. Subsequently, however, it was decided to dissolve the political functions of the UAM, while retaining the economic aspects of the organization already operating. The name of the new group is the Union Afro-Malgache de Coopération Economique.

The experience with regional federations up to the present time would appear to indicate that they came into existence not so much as a means of fostering African unification as to serve the more immediate political interests of the governments concerned. When these interests were no longer compatible or when the federation had served the internal political purpose for which it was created, it was apt to disappear from the scene. President Nyerere of Tanganyika, for example, used the prospect of East African federation to encourage the British government to hasten the grant of independence to Uganda and Kenya, the other two potential members of such a federation. When, however, this immediate purpose had been served and the other two states became independent, other political conditions created by the new relationships of independence (such as Uganda's fear of economic domination by Kenya) worked to postpone the immediate creation of the new federation. PAFMECSA, on the other hand, has been dissolved, because the Committee of Nine of the OAU assumed its function as the leader of the southern African liberation movements.

It is, of course, easy to extend almost indefinitely the list of obstacles to African unity, but the fact of the presence of these obstacles should not blind the outside observer of the African political scene to the immense importance of pan-Africanism as a moving force in Africa today, particularly among the younger generation of leaders who are maturing within the present governing parties of the new states. The emotional appeal of the symbols of pan-African unity and African brotherhood are very great, and the dream of a continent united under one government, which would speak for the people of Africa with a powerful voice in international political circles, is much more attractive than the present loose and often discordant voices of Africa. For the youth groups, who are the next generation of African leaders, in those countries where more conservative nationalist governments have not so emphatically asserted African independence in their relationship to the former mother countries, President Nkrumah's brand of political pan-Africanism is much more significant than the gradualism developing out of a growing identity of economic interests that was the theme of most of the older leaders at Addis Ababa. Pan-Africanist political unity has become not only an emotional slogan for the younger intellectuals but has also been, particularly in Nigeria, a platform for the opposition upon which to oppose the government on foreign policy.

Pan-Africanism, with its emphasis on the African personality, the individuality of African values, and the restoration of the dignity of Africans in the eyes of the world, has had profound effects on both the foreign and domestic policies of the African states. On the level of foreign policy, it has inevitably initiated a trend toward semi-isolationism. The desire to assert an independent role for the African community of states, the need to demonstrate a clear break with the former colonial power (of which the severing of ties with the British Crown by the creation of republics in

Nigeria, Ghana and Tanganyika is symptomatic), and the effort to assume a neutralist stance in the East-West conflict, as well as the creation of an independent "African" ideology — African socialism — have all led to a distinctiveness of the African states in world affairs, but have also in some degree tended to isolate them from the main currents of world politics.

Another effect of pan-Africanism has also been a greater degree of authoritarianism in the internal policies of some African states. The militant pan-Africanist groups who favor the predominance of political pan-Africanism tend to be in the opposition in the more moderate countries. Their efforts to force the adoption of policies on African unity which correspond more closely to the Ghanaian point of view has left them open to the accusation of plotting against the security of the state because their efforts are seen as being supported from the outside. The plot of which the Action Group Party in Nigeria was accused in 1962 and which resulted in the trial of the leader of the opposition, Obafemi Awolowo, on charges of treason is typical of this phenomenon. At the time, evidence was produced to indicate that the Ghanaian government was giving at least indirect support to the Nigerian opposition plotters. The reaction of some governments toward what they have assumed to be an external threat stemming from a militant pan-Africanism has been to label the opposition as traitors and to press for more authoritarian suppression of the opposition on this ground.

With the stress that pan-Africanism lays on building a self-reliant and independent economy and the need for the full mobilization of society to work toward this goal, encouragement is lent to the establishment of monolithic political structures of the "guided democracy" type displaying heavy elements of authoritarianism. The political style set by the PDG in Guinea and the CPP in Ghana have become the models which the new generation of African leaders seek to emulate. Pan-Africanism calls for the embracing of the single doctrine of African socialism by all African countries, and by its very nature it seeks to make the African countries more uniform in their political structures so that they may better fit into a united whole. Inevitably, the leveling influences derived from pan-Africanism and African socialism as an ideology for the mobilization of the masses in pursuit of specific economic goals will mean greater pressure toward the creation of a single African community, but a community which will be able to take little cognizance of the cultural differences which exist within it. While this may in the long run make for greater African unity, it may also have the effect of deadening African individualism both on a national and a personal basis.

The evolution of pan-Africanism from a program of political action which was essentially anti-imperialist and anti-colonialist to an expression of nationalist ambitions favoring a grand strategy of all African countries in the formation of a semi-monolithic African community reflects the gradual and subtle changes which are taking place in the viewpoints of the African governments as they begin to realize the full implications of independence. It remains to be seen, however, whether the appeal of a pan-Africanism aimed at a wider federation of African states united under a single political structure can triumph over the long pull in the face of the growing counterpull of the individual national interests involved.

African Unity and the Non-African World

The differing views on the best road to unity in Africa held by the Casablanca and the Monrovia groups have been reflected in the postures taken by the African states in their relations with outside powers. On many points of foreign policy, they have been largely in agreement. Without exception, they favor the liberation of all of Africa and, where necessary, assistance to the liberation movements in the areas which still remain under European control or, as in the case of South Africa, under the control of a Government which subjugates the interests of the African population to those of the European. All insist on decolonization, but they are not necessarily always united on the question of the rate at which the process should take place. Some African powers, such as Ghana and Guinea, have urged that complete decolonization take place by a specific date; the majority, however, accept the point of view that, while it should take place as rapidly as possible, not all areas are at the same stage of development and therefore no final timetable can be laid down.

The definition of the role of the independent states as supporters of national liberation movements has created a major area of disagreement. The Casablanca powers favored full support by the African bloc for the provisional government of Algeria in the struggle against the French administration. The UAM, on the other hand, pressed for continued negotiation between the French government and the Algerian leadership but was not prepared to take a firm stand at the United Nations to force the capitulation of France to the demands of the Algerian nationalists. Similarly, in the case of the Congo, a split developed between the African powers. The Casablanca group strongly favored the regime of Patrice Lumumba, and maintained that the military action of the United Nations in the Congo was contrary to the interests of self-determination in Africa. They saw in the continued existence of the dissident province of Katanga a surrender of the African nationalist movement to the interests of the imperialist powers. Because the United Nations Command failed to meet their demand for immediate expulsion of the Tshombe regime and was able neither to protect Lumumba's life nor to maintain his government in power, the organization was condemned by the Casablanca powers. The more moderate Monrovia group of African states continued to give support to the United Nations forces in the Congo and to the policies of the Secretary-General. The Congo issue was the most serious point of disagreement among the African powers since independence. For the first time it became clear how divisive could be the effect on the new countries of the injection of the cold war into Africa.

The African states did not always see eye to eye on the question of their relations with their former colonial powers. The military pacts signed between the African countries and the former metropolitan governments after independence became a contested issue between the more extreme nationalist governments such as Guinea, which favored a total break with the former colonial power, and the governments of other French-speaking states which felt that at the present stage of development protection by French troops was still necessary to insure their survival as independent states since they were financially incapable of creating the armed forces necessary for their own protection. Even within a single country, Nigeria, the question of the continuing military relationship with Great Britain was a source of strife. The pact which had been contracted with Britain as part of the independence settlement was cited by the opposition Action Group in debates on foreign policy in the Nigerian Federal Parliament as proof that the majority party was still subservient to British interests, and after student rioting in the Parliament building itself, the Government finally agreed to abrogate the pact.

On the question of neutralism and non-alignment the African powers have been in general agreement, although here again the "degree" of neutrality has been in dispute. The so-called "extreme" nationalists, Ghana, Guinea and Mali, joined with Morocco and the UAR in pressing for a stand of absolute neutrality on the part of the African bloc in the cold war. The African representatives at the Belgrade Conference of Neutralist Powers, convened by Yugoslavia in 1961, insisted that the real proof of African independence lay in adherence to the principle of complete non-alignment. Because of their past relationships with the Western powers, the adoption of a position of "positive neutralism" inevitably meant that the extreme neutralists more frequently took public positions at the United Nations and elsewhere which opposed the views of the Western powers while failing to make as evident their genuine neutrality in regard to the actions of the Eastern bloc. At the Belgrade Conference, for example; atomic warfare was roundly condemned but the Conference failed to take a stand opposing the Soviet resumption of atomic testing. The more moderate neutralists of the Monrovia, and particularly the UAM, groups have not found it necessary to reaffirm their position by a consistently anti-Western stand.

The interpretation of the content of a genuinely neutralist position has become a point of disagreement between the two major groups of African states. The Casablanca powers maintain that any substantial measure of agreement with the position of the West implies a commitment and hence a betrayal of the African neutralist position. The Monrovia group proved to be somewhat more realistic in the meaning they attach to neutrality. One of their representatives argued:

> In the political domain, neutralism is an illusion. Politics consists in taking sides. One cannot be neutral before the problem of peace, disarmament, or the development of the underdeveloped areas.... One must take a stand on every international problem.... The essential point, however, is not to systematically take a stand for one or the other of the two blocs which dispute their control of the world.... Neutralism or non-alignment, or non-engagement, corresponds directly to the common desire to safeguard one's independence and one's liberty of action. The real question is: is such a policy possible for the young states of Africa?[4]

Complete neutrality, the moderates point out, is not possible for developing areas such as the African states because they are dependent in so many ways on aid from outside sources. Genuine independence and resistance to neo-colonialism, they insist, is not proved by consistently voting in the United Nations against the West, but by an evaluation of the national interest on each issue upon which

---

[4]Thiam, *op. cit.*, pp. 106-7.

they are required to take a position, and voting according to this interest. If this demands agreement with the Western position, it by no means follows that a relationship of subservience to the Western powers is thus created.

To the African governments, as to others in the developing areas, membership in the United Nations has been of immense value in the formation of foreign policy. It has provided them with a forum in which they may express their views on world issues, and in so doing they further reinforce international acceptance of their independence. Because their votes count in the determination of the position of the United Nations, they draw from it psychological support for their determination to be regarded as equals in the community of states. Although they draw limited material help for economic modernization from the international body, the most important attribute of United Nations membership lies, for the African countries particularly, in the realm of the spirit.

Through coordination of their views on questions arising in the United Nations, the members of the Afro-Asian bloc can, by means of Assembly resolutions, exercise effective pressure on the policies of the great powers. The realization of the power inherent in a common stand at the international level tends to be a unifying factor within the African community of states, and to some extent may offset the divisions that national interests create within the continent itself. The individual national vote at the United Nations continues to be a cherished sign of the recognition of sovereignty. But the expression of unity born of a cooperative effort to serve the interests of each at the international level may in the long run be a more solid foundation for an African community than Kwame Nkrumah's dream of political federation in Africa could ever have been.

Part II
Reference

Compiled by Annette E. Stiefbold

Reference section designed by Witt-Francis Associates and produced by Maryart Studio

Table of Contents

Economy

Government Expenditure under Development Plans
Regional Comparison of Per Capita GNP
Per Capita GNP in Selected African Countries (map)
Per Capita National Income
Employment in Non-Agricultural Activities
Regional Comparison of Vehicles in Use
Miles of Railroad Tracks in Selected African Countries
Production of Cement of Selected African Countries
Production of Electricity of Selected African Countries
Hydro-Electric Power Projects (map)

Commerce

Pattern of African Foreign Trade
Africa's Customers and Suppliers
Africa's Share of World Trade
Principal Exports of Selected African Countries
Intra-African Trade of Selected West African
Countries

Aid

United Nations Technical Assistance to Africa
Projects of the United Nations Special Fund in Africa
World Bank Aid to Africa
Communist Bloc Aid to Africa
United States Government Aid to Africa
European Development Fund Aid to Africa
Bilateral Assistance to Selected African Countries

SEARCH FOR UNITY

French African Federations
Inter-African and Malagasy States Organization
East African Common Services Organization
Organization of African Unity
Council of the Entente
Pan-African Freedom Movement of East, Central and
    Southern Africa
Casablanca Group
Union of African States and Madagascar

APPENDIX PREFACE

The Appendix which follows is a compilation of information of general interest concerning three broad areas of African reality: society, economy, and polity. Its purpose is to make accessible and meaningful frequently needed statistical information which is normally difficult either to obtain or to interpret. This brief survey is by no means exhaustive. The intention is rather to present a general overview of contemporary Africa. Additional material on particular subjects often can be found by consulting the sources indicated.

I. Introduction to Africa

Events in Africa often occur with such rapidity that it is impossible for the observant layman to keep abreast of them. An understanding of contemporary Africa is facilitated by a general familiarity both with the colonial past and with the post-independence structure and leadership. This introduction identifies people, places, and events, for ready reference in analyzing contemporary developments on the African continent.

Independent Nations of Africa

Short Form	Long Form	Noun/ Adjective Form
Algeria	Democratic and Popular Republic of Algeria	Algerian
Burundi	Kingdom of Burundi	Burundian
Cameroon	Federal Republic of Cameroon	Cameroonian
. . . . . .	Central African Republic	Central African
Chad	Republic of Chad	Chadien, Chadian
Congo	Republic of Congo (Brazzaville)	Congolese, Congo
Congo	Republic of the Congo (Leopoldville)	Congolese, Congo
Dahomey	Republic of Dahomey	Dahomean
Ethiopia	Empire of Ethiopia	Ethiopian
Gabon	Gabon Republic	Gabonese
Ghana	Republic of Ghana	Ghanaian
Guinea	Republic of Guinea	Guinean
Ivory Coast	Republic of Ivory Coast	Ivoirian, Ivoirien
Kenya	No long form designated	Kenyan
Liberia	Republic of Liberia	Liberian
Libya	Kingdom of Libya	Libyan

Independent Nations of Africa

Short Form	Long Form	Noun/ Adjective Form
Madagascar	Malagasy Republic	Malagasy
Malawi	No long form designated	Malawian
Mali	Republic of Mali	Malian
Mauritania	Islamic Republic of Mauritania	Mauritanian
Morocco	Kingdom of Morocco	Moroccan
Niger	Republic of Niger	Nigerois (noun), Niger (adjective)
Nigeria	Republic of Nigeria	Nigerian
Rwanda	Republic of Rwanda	Rwandan (noun), Rwanda (adjective)
Senegal	Republic of Senegal	Senegalese, Senegal
Sierra Leone	No long form designated	Sierra Leonean
Somalia	Somali Republic	Somali
South Africa	Republic of South Africa	South African
Sudan	Republic of the Sudan	Sudanese
Tanganyika	Republic of Tanganyika	Tanganyikan
Togo	Republic of Togo	Togolese
Tunisia	Republic of Tunisia	Tunisian
Uganda	No long form designated	Ugandan (noun), Uganda (adjective)
Upper Volta	Republic of Upper Volta	Upper Voltan (noun), Upper Volta (adj.)
. . . . . .	United Arab Republic[1]	(Egyptian)
Zambia	Republic of Zambia	Zambian
Zanzibar	People's Republic of Zanzibar	Zanzibari

Dependent Areas

	Dependency of	Status
Angola (includes Cabinda)	Portugal	Province
Basutoland	Britain	High Commission Territory
Bechuanaland	Britain	High Commission Territory
Cape Verde Islands	Portugal	Province
Comoro Islands	France	Overseas Territory
Couta	Spain	Plaza
French Somaliland	France	Overseas Territory
Gambia	Britain	Colony and Protectorate
Ifni	Spain	Province
Mauritius	Britain	Colony
Melilla	Spain	Plaza
Portuguese Guinea	Portugal	Province
Réunion	France	Overseas Department
Sao Tome & Principe	Portugal	Province
Southern Rhodesia	Britain	Self-Governing Colony[2]
South-West Africa	South Africa	League of Nations Mandate, Class C[3]
Spanish Guinea (Fernando Po, Rio Muni)	Spain	Provinces (autonomous)
Spanish Sahara	Spain	Province
Swaziland	Britain	High Commission Territory

[1] No short form exists for United Arab Republic, although the initials U.A.R. are sometimes used. "Egypt" in parentheses often appears in conjunction with the official name.

[2] Juridical status, although the designation as "colony" was officially dropped in 1964.

[3] Status disputed; case pending before International Court of Justice.

Source: Adapted from Status of the World's Nations, Geographic Bulletin No. 2, U.S. Department of State; Profiles of Newly Independent States, U.S. Department of State.

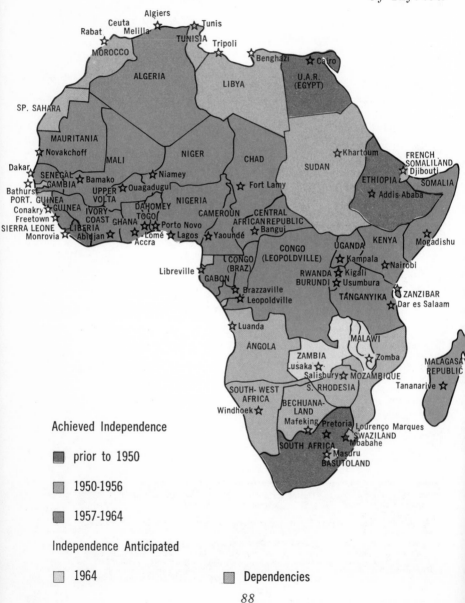

*The Independent
Nations
of Africa*

Achieved Independence

■ prior to 1950

■ 1950-1956

■ 1957-1964

Independence Anticipated

■ 1964   ■ Dependencies

88

The Advent
of Independence

Symbols:
Member of French Com.
Associated with Fr. Com.
Member Brit. Commonwealth

Country	Date of Independence	Remarks	Present Chief of State
Ethiopia		Independent throughout its 3,000-year history except for brief period of Italian occupation, 1936-41.	Emperor Haile Selassie I
Liberia	1847	Organized in 1823 by American missionaries for freed slaves from the United States.	President William V. S. Tubman
Egypt (UAR)	1922	Ruled by Ottoman Empire, France, Britain. Recently joined with other Arab states in loose unions.	President Gamal Abdel Nasser
South Africa	1931	Former Union of South Africa became independent under the Statute of Westminster in 1931. Became a Republic in 1961 and withdrew from Commonwealth.	President Charles Robberts Swart
Libya	Dec. 24, 1951	Conquered by Italy before World War II. First country to obtain independence through direct United Nations action.	King Muhammad Idris al-Mahdi al-Sanusi
Sudan*	Jan. 1, 1956	Joint Anglo-Egyptian administration until independence.	General Ibrahim Abboud
Morocco	Mar. 2, 1956	French protectorate since 1912. French forced to restore deposed King Mohammed V and grant independence after continued threats of violence.	King Hassan II

*Sudan, lying astride the line separating North Africa from the southern segment of the continent, culturally belongs to the north.
[1] In April 1964 these two countries merged to form the United Republic of Tanganyika and Zanzibar, with Julius Nyerere as President and Abeid Karume as a Vice President.

Country	Date of Independence	Remarks	Present Chief of State
Tunisia	Mar. 20, 1956	Former Barbary state under Turkey. French protectorate from 1881. With Morocco, pressed for and obtained independence from France.	President Habib Bourguiba
Ghana	Mar. 6, 1957	Former British Gold Coast. First sub-Saharan African country to achieve independence in the twentieth century.*	President Kwame Nkrumah
Guinea	Oct. 2, 1958	Voted "no" to General de Gaulle's offer of association with French Community. Only French African territory to do so. Resulted in total break with France, now mending.	President Sekou Touré
Cameroon	Jan. 1, 1960	Former German colony. League of Nations then United Nations mandate, part administered by France, part by Britain. French mandate became independent republic, joined by southern part of British mandate.	President Ahmadou Ahidjo
Togo	Apr. 27, 1960	Former French Togoland. United Nations Trust Territory (former German colony).	President Nicolas Grunitzky
Madagascar	June 26, 1960	French protectorate since 1885.	President Philibert Tsiranana
Congo (Leopoldville)	June 30, 1960	Personal territory of King Leopold of Belgium. In 1908 transferred to Belgian government. Independence followed by total collapse of central authority.	President Joseph Kasavubu
Somalia	July 1, 1960	Composed of (1) Italian Somaliland, former UN trust territory, which became independent July 1, 1960; and (2) British Somaliland, which became independent June 26, 1960.	President Aden Abdullah Osman

Country	Date of Independence	Remarks	Present Chief of State
Dahomey	Aug. 1, 1960	Former autonomous republic within French Community. Independence proclaimed following accord with France.	President Sourou Migan Apithy
Niger	Aug. 3, 1960	Former autonomous republic within French Community. Independence proclaimed following accord with France.	President Hamani Diori
Upper Volta	Aug. 5, 1960	Former autonomous republic within French Community. Independence proclaimed following accord with France.	President Maurice Yameogo
Ivory Coast	Aug. 7, 1960	Former autonomous republic within French Community. Independence proclaimed following accord with France.	President Felix Houphouet-Boigny
Chad	Aug. 11, 1960	Former autonomous republic within French Community. Independence proclaimed following accord with France.	President François Tombalbaye
Central African Repub.	Aug. 13, 1960	Former autonomous republic within French Community. Independence proclaimed following accord with France. Former Ubangi-Shari.	President David Dacko
Congo (Brazzaville)	Aug. 15, 1960	Former autonomous republic within French Community. Independence proclaimed following accord with France. Former Middle Congo.	President Alphonse Massamba-Debat
Gabon	Aug. 17, 1960	Former autonomous republic within French Community. Independence proclaimed following accord with France.	President Leon M'ba

Country	Date of Independence	Remarks	Present Chief of State
Mali	Sept. 24, 1960	Former French Sudan, autonomous republic within French Community. Joined Senegal in Mali Federation, June 1960. When Senegal withdrew, kept name of Mali.	President Modibo Keita
Senegal	Sept. 24, 1960	See above.	President Leopold Sedar Senghor
Nigeria	Oct. 1, 1960	Former colony and protectorate under British administration Joined by Northern Cameroons, British Trust Territory, in 1961 after plebiscite.	President Nnamdi Azikiwe
Mauritania	Nov. 28, 1960	Former autonomous republic within French Community.	President Moktar Ould Daddah
Sierra Leone	Apr. 27, 1961	Former colony and protectorate under British administration.	Queen Elizabeth II, represented by Governor-General Sir Henry Lightfoot Boston. (Head of government is Albert Margai.)
Tanganyika	Dec. 9, 1961	Former German East Africa. Became British Trust Territory in 1919, under League of Nations. Became United Nations Trust Territory under British administration in 1946.	President Julius Nyerere
Burundi	July 1, 1962	Former United Nations Trust Territory administered by Belgium together with Rwanda, as Rwanda-Urundi.	Mwami Mwambutsa IV

Country	Date of Independence	Remarks	Present Chief of State
Rwanda	July 1, 1962	See above.	President Gregoire Kayibanda
Algeria	July 3, 1962	Juridically considered part of France until independence after protracted rebellion, which began in 1954.	President Ahmed Ben Bella
Uganda	Oct. 9, 1962	Former British protectorate.	President, Sir Edward Mutesa II, the Kabaka of Buganda
Zanzibar[1]	Dec. 10, 1963	Former British protectorate.	President Abeid Karume[1]
Kenya	Dec. 12, 1963	Former British colony and protectorate. Opposition to British highlighted by Mau Mau rebellion.	Queen Elizabeth II, represented by Governor-General Malcolm MacDonald. (Head of government is Jomo Kenyatta.)
Malawi	July 6, 1964	Former British protectorate of Nyasaland, former member of Federation of Rhodesia and Nyasaland.	Queen Elizabeth II, represented by Governor Sir Evelyn Hone. (Head of government is Hastings Banda.)
Zambia	Oct. 24, 1964	Former British protectorate of Northern Rhodesia, former member of Federation of Rhodesia and Nyasaland.	President Kenneth Kaunda

MAJOR PORTS AND RAILWAY NETWORK

||||||||||||||Railroads

☆ Major Ports (1 million tons or more annually)

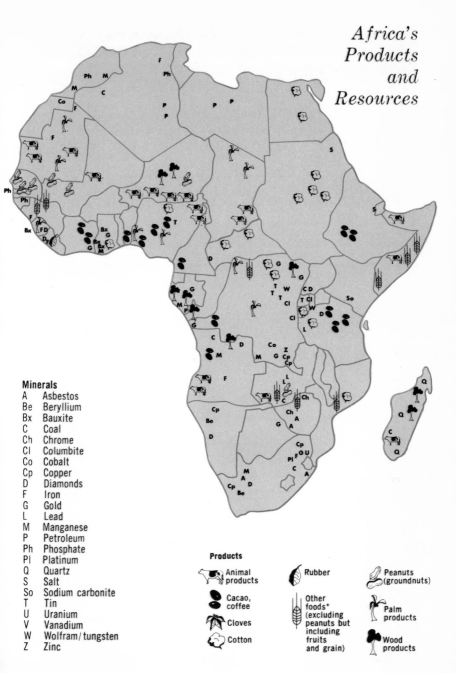

Africa's
Products
and
Resources

Minerals

A   Asbestos
Be Beryllium
Bx Bauxite
C   Coal
Ch Chrome
Cl Columbite
Co Cobalt
Cp Copper
D   Diamonds
F   Iron
G   Gold
L   Lead
M   Manganese
P   Petroleum
Ph Phosphate
Pl Platinum
Q   Quartz
S   Salt
So Sodium carbonite
T   Tin
U   Uranium
V   Vanadium
W   Wolfram/tungsten
Z   Zinc

Products

Animal products

Cacao, coffee

Cloves

Cotton

Rubber

Other foods* (excluding peanuts but including fruits and grain)

Peanuts (groundnuts)

Palm products

Wood products

Principal African Political Parties[1]

Country	Party	Leader
Algeria	National Liberation Front (FLN)*	Ahmed Ben Bella
Angola	Front for the National Liberation of Angola (FLNA)	Holden Roberto
	Popular Liberation Movement of Angola (MPLA)	Mario de Andrade, Agostinho Neto
Basutoland	Basutoland Congress Party	Ntsu Mokhehle
	Basutoland Freedom Party	Motlotlehi Moshoeshoe
Bechuanaland	Bechuanaland Democratic Party	Seretse Khama
	Bechuanaland People's Party	Kgalemani Motsete
Burundi	National Union for Progress (UPRONA)	Pierre Ngendandumwe
Cameroon	Cameroonian Union	Ahmadou Ahidjo
	Kamerun National Democratic Party	John Ngu Foncha
Cape Verde Islands	Liberation Movement of Cape Verde (MLCV)	Mendes Diaz
	Union of the People of the Cape Verde Islands	Jose Laitao de Groca
	African Party for the Independence of Guinea and Cape Verde (PAIGC)	Amilcar Cabral

Country	Party	Leader
Central African Republic	Movement for the Social Emancipation of Black Africa (MESAN)*	David Dacko
Chad	Chadien Progressive Party (PPT)*	François Tombalbaye
Congo (Brazzaville)	National Movement of the Revolution (provisional government party)*	
Congo (Leopoldville)	"Binza group" (governmental and administrative officials now seeking to form political party)	Justin Bomboko, Victor Nendaka, Joseph D. Mobotu
	Many splinter political movements, including: Alliance of the Bakongo (ABAKO)	
	African Solidarity Party (PSA)	Gizenga and Kamitatu factions
	Congolese National Movement-Lumumba (MNC-L)	
Dahomey	Dahomean Democratic Party (PDD)*	Gabriel Lozes
Ethiopia	None	
Gabon	Gabonese Democratic Block (BDG)	Leon M'ba
Gambia	People's Progressive Party (PPP)	David K. Jawara
	United Party	P. S. N'Jie
	Democratic Congress Alliance	Garba-Jahumpa
Ghana	Convention People's Party (CPP)*	Kwame Nkrumah
Guinea	Democratic Party of Guinea (PDG)*	Sekou Touré

Country	Party	Leader
Ivory Coast	Democratic Party of the Ivory Coast (PDCI)*	Felix Houphouet-Boigny
Kenya	Kenya African National Union (KANU) Kenya African Democratic Union (KADU)	Jomo Kenyatta Ronald Ngala
Liberia	True Whig Party*	William V. S. Tubman
Libya	None	
Malagasy Republic	Social Democratic Party Ankoton'ny Kongresi'ny Fahaleovantenan Madagasikara (AKFAM)	Philibert Tsiranana
Malawi	Malawi Congress Party*	Hastings Kamuzu Banda
Mali	Sudanese Union (US)*	Modibo Keita
Mauritania	Party of the People (PDP)*	Moktar Ould Daddah
Mozambique	Front for the Liberation of Mozambique (FRELIMO) National Democratic Union of Mozambique (UDENAMO) Mozambique African United Front	Eduardo Mondlane Paul Gumane Mathew Mmole, Adelino Gwambe

Country	Party	Leader
Morocco	Front for the Defense of the Constitutional Institutions (FDIC)	Ahmad Rheda Guedira
	Istiqlal (Independence Party)	Allal al-Fassi
	National Union of Popular Forces (UNFP)	El Mehdi Ben Barka, Abderrahim Bouabid
Niger	Niger Progressive Party (PPN)	Hamani Diori
	Sawaba Party (banned)	Djibo Bakary
Nigeria	National Council of Nigerian Citizens (NCNC)	Michael I. Okpara
	Northern People's Congress (NPC)	Alhaji Sir Ahmadu Bello
	Action Group (AG)	Obafemi Awolowo (imprisoned)
	United People's Party	Samuel L. Akintola
Portuguese Guinea	African Party for the Independence of Guinea and Cape Verde (PAIGC)	Amilcar Cabral
	Front for the National Independence Struggle of Guinea (FLING)	
	Movement for the Liberation of So-called Portuguese Guinea	François Mendy
Rwanda	Republican Party of the Movement for the Emancipation of the Hutu (PARMEHUTU)	Gregoire Kayibanda
Senegal	Senegalese Progressive Union (UPS)*	Leopold Sedar Senghor
	Party of African Regroupment (PRA)	Abdoulaye Ly
Sierra Leone	Sierra Leone People's Party (SLPP)	Albert Margai
	All People's Congress (APC)	Siaka Stevens

Country	Party	Leader
Somali Republic	Somali Youth League (SYL)	Yassin Nur Hassan
	Somali National Congress (SNC) Somali Democratic Union (SDU)	
South Africa	National Party	Hendrik F. Verwoerd
	United Party	Sir de Villiers Graaf
	Progressive Party	Jan Steytler
	Liberal Party	Alan Paton
	African National Congress (banned)	Albert J. Luthuli
	Pan-Africanist Congress (banned)	Robert Sobukwe Potlako Leballo
Southern Rhodesia	Rhodesian Front	Ian Smith
	Rhodesia National Party	Sir Edgar Whitehead
	Peoples Caretaker Council	Joshua Nkomo
	Zimbabwe Africa National Union (ZANU)	Ndabaningi Sithole
South-West Africa	National Party	J.G.H. Vanderwath
	United National South-West Party	J. P. Niehaus
	South-West Africa People's Organization (SWAPO)	Sam Nujoma (in exile)
	South-West African National Union (SWANU)	Jarietundu Kozonguizi
Sudan	None	
Swaziland	Swaziland Progressive Party	J. J. Nquku
	Ngwane National Liberatory Congress (NNLB)	Ambrose P. Zwane
	Swaziland Democratic Party	Simon Nxumalo

Country	Party	Leader
Tanganyika	Tanganyika African National Union (TANU)*	Julius Nyerere
Togo	Democratic Union of Togolese Populations (UDPT)	Idrissou Antoine Meatchi
	Party of Togolese Unity (PUT)	
	Movement of Togolese Youth (JUVENTO)	Anani Santos
	Togolese Popular Movement (MPT)	Abdelmajed Chaker
Tunisia	Neo-Destour	Habib Bourguiba (honorary)
Uganda	Uganda People's Congress (UPC)	Milton Obote, G. Ibingira
	Kabaka Yekka	Sir Edward Mutesa II
	Democratic Party	Benedicto Kiwanuka, Basil Bataringaya
United Arab Republic	Arab Socialist Union	Gamal Abdel Nasser
Upper Volta	Voltan Democratic Union (UDV)*	Maurice Yameogo
Zambia	United National Independence Party (UNIP)	Kenneth Kaunda
	African National Congress (ANC)	Harry Nkumbula
Zanzibar	Afro-Shirazi Party*	Abeid Karume

[1] *Includes banned opposition and exiled parties.*
Indicates single party or single dominant party.

II. Society and Culture

The continent of Africa is the home of many peoples who differ from one another with respect to language, history, customs and physical characteristics. Not long ago such differences were largely disregarded by the general public and colonial administrators. The grouping of heterogenous tribes into administrative units both laid the foundation for the emergence of the new nations of Africa and gave rise to problems of national integration and identity which confront these nations today. An added factor which has contributed to the disintegration of traditional society and its reintegration within larger national units has been the African exposure to non-indigenous elements such as white settlers, missionaries, and traders. The presence of whites intensified resentment against the inequalities inherent in the colonial situation. The work of missionaries in propagating ideas of equality and in providing Western education supplied both the moral justification for revolt against colonialism and the cultural tool for achieving equality. On the other hand, the role of the Arab traders in helping to spread the Islamic faith, served the cause of nationalism by providing an integrative force as an alternative to the Christianity of the colonial regime.

One of the factors complicating efforts to improve the material well-being of the African peoples is the great disparity in regional population distribution. The difficulties of providing services in areas of extremely low population density (e.g., Bechuanaland, Libya), are matched by land shortage problems in areas of high density (e.g. Zanzibar, Nyasaland). Furthermore, although Africa is overwhelmingly agricultural, it does not produce food in large enough quantity or variety to feed its people. Finally, the acute shortage of medical facilities accounts for the loss of much human energy through debilitating diseases.

Making education available to all of its youth is one of the greatest challenges facing Africa today. The inadequacy of present educational facilities to meet the requirements of economic and social development is shown by a regional comparison of literacy, a survey of existing educational establishments, and school attendance. The desire for knowledge and exposure to new ideas also is reflected in the rise of newspaper circulation.

Major Ethnic Groups of Africa

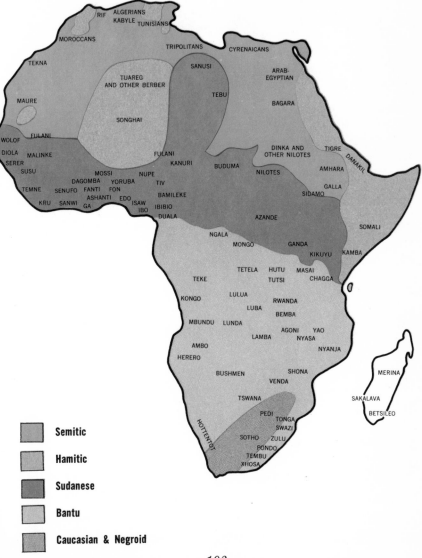

Semitic

Hamitic

Sudanese

Bantu

Caucasian & Negroid

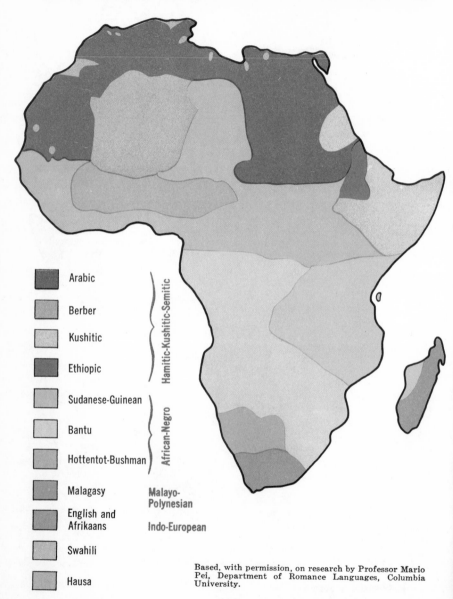

Major Linguistic Regions of Africa

Arabic

Berber

Kushitic

Ethiopic

Hamitic-Kushitic-Semitic

Sudanese-Guinean

Bantu

Hottentot-Bushman

African-Negro

Malagasy — Malayo-Polynesian

English and Afrikaans — Indo-European

Swahili

Hausa

Based, with permission, on research by Professor Mario Pei, Department of Romance Languages, Columbia University.

104

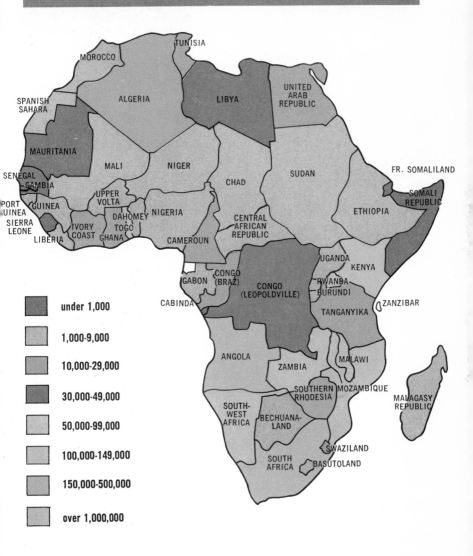

White Residents in Africa As of 1962*

Legend:
- under 1,000
- 1,000-9,000
- 10,000-29,000
- 30,000-49,000
- 50,000-99,000
- 100,000-149,000
- 150,000-500,000
- over 1,000,000

Map labels: TUNISIA, MOROCCO, SPANISH SAHARA, ALGERIA, LIBYA, UNITED ARAB REPUBLIC, MAURITANIA, MALI, NIGER, CHAD, SUDAN, FR. SOMALILAND, SENEGAL, GAMBIA, PORT. GUINEA, GUINEA, SIERRA LEONE, LIBERIA, IVORY COAST, UPPER VOLTA, GHANA, TOGO, DAHOMEY, NIGERIA, CAMEROUN, CENTRAL AFRICAN REPUBLIC, ETHIOPIA, SOMALI REPUBLIC, GABON, CONGO (BRAZ), CONGO (LEOPOLDVILLE), CABINDA, UGANDA, KENYA, RWANDA, BURUNDI, TANGANYIKA, ZANZIBAR, ANGOLA, ZAMBIA, MALAWI, MOZAMBIQUE, SOUTHERN RHODESIA, MALAGASY REPUBLIC, SOUTH-WEST AFRICA, BECHUANALAND, SWAZILAND, SOUTH AFRICA, BASUTOLAND

*Figure for Algeria represents post-independence departure of many white settlers. Prior to independence there were over 1 million white settlers there.

The Spread of Non-Indigenous Religions in Africa

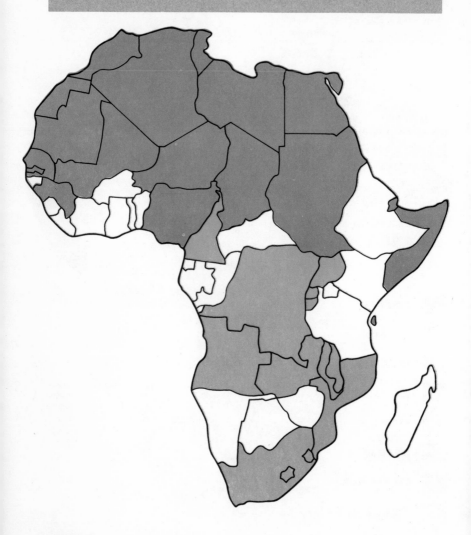

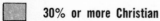 30% or more Christian

50% or more Moslem

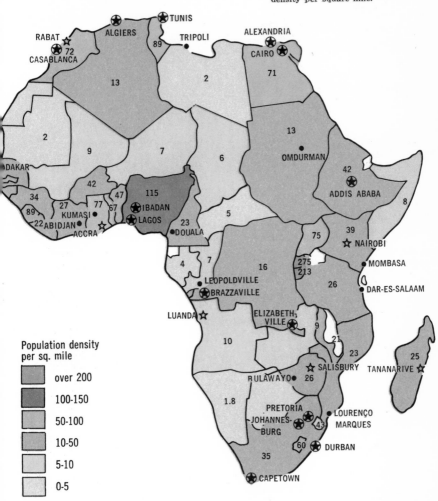

Population Distribution & Urbanization

*The numbers within each country indicate the precise population density per square mile.

RABAT ☆
CASABLANCA ● 72
ALGIERS ☆
TUNIS ☆
89 TRIPOLI
ALEXANDRIA
CAIRO ☆
71
13
2
DAKAR
2
9
7
6
13
OMDURMAN
42 ☆
ADDIS ABABA
8
34
42
47
115
27 77 67 ● IBADAN
89 KUMASI ● ☆ LAGOS
22 ABIDJAN ●
ACCRA
23
DOUALA ●
5
75
39
☆ NAIROBI
MOMBASA ●
DAR-ES-SALAAM ●
4 7
16
275
213
26
LEOPOLDVILLE ☆
BRAZZAVILLE ☆
LUANDA ☆
10
ELIZABETH-VILLE ☆
9
21
23
25
SALISBURY ☆
BULAWAYO ● 26
TANANARIVE ☆
1.8
PRETORIA ☆
JOHANNES-BURG ☆
43
LOURENÇO MARQUES ●
60 ☆ DURBAN
35
CAPETOWN ☆

Population density per sq. mile

- over 200
- 100-150
- 50-100
- 10-50
- 5-10
- 0-5

Cities and towns

- ☆ over 300,000
- ☆ 200,000-300,000
- ● 100,000-200,000

Source: Agency for International Development. Statistics and Reports Division. *Selected Economic Data for the Less Developed Countries.* May 1963.

The Population of Africa in 1962

Country	Total Mill.	Rate of Growth (per cent)	% Urban of Total Pop. (in towns of 10,000 or more)
Algeria	11.5	2.5	n.a.
Angola	4.8	1.2	11 (1950)
Basutoland	0.7	1.7	n.a.
Bechuanaland	0.3	1.6	14 (est.)
Burundi	2.3	2.1	1
Cameroon	4.2	1.0	n.a.
Central African Republic	1.3	1.8	12
Chad	3.0	2.5	4 (3% of African pop., 64% of non-African pop.)
Congo (Braz.)	0.9	2.6	21.4
Congo (Leo.)	14.8	2.5	9 (8.7% of African pop., 61.8% of non-African pop.)
Dahomey	2.1	2.8	10
Ethiopia	19.4	1.4	n.a.
Gabon	0.4	0.8	9 (towns of 5,000 or more)
Gambia	0.3	0.7	n.a.
Ghana	7.1	2.5	17
Guinea	3.2	3.0	6 (1958)
Ivory Coast	3.4	2.3	8
Kenya	8.7	3.0	8 (est.)
Liberia	1.0	1.5	n.a.
Libya	1.2	1.5	30
Madagascar	5.7	2.7	9
Malawi	3.2	2.5	n.a.
Mali	4.3	2.0	3 (3% of African pop., 64% of non-African pop.)
Mauritania	0.7	3.7	2 (1955; towns of 5,000 or more)
Mauritius	0.7	3.2	n.a.
Morocco	12.3	3.0	29.3
Mozambique	6.7	1.5	23.0
Niger	3.2	2.7	2
Nigeria	41.0	2.0	19 (towns of 5,000 or more)
Rwanda	2.8	3.2	1
Senegal	3.1	2.5	19
Sierra Leone	2.5	1.9	5 (towns of 9,000 or more)
Somalia	2.0	0.9	n.a.
South Africa	16.7	2.6	33 (1951; 25% of non-white pop., 62% of white pop.)
Southern Rhodesia	3.9	3.0	20 (15% of African pop., 73% of European pop.)

Country	Total Mill.	Rate of Growth (per cent)	% Urban of Total Pop. (in towns of 10,000 or more)
South-West Africa	0.6	n.a.	n.a.
Sudan	12.4	2.8	4 (1955-56)
Swaziland	0.3	3.2	n.a.
Tanganyika	9.6	1.8	3 (2% of African pop., 40% of European pop., 74% of Indian-Pakistani pop., 38% of other groups)
Togo	1.5	3.0	n.a.
Tunisia	4.3	2.2	34
U.A.R. (Egypt)	27.3	2.5	33
Uganda	7.0	2.5	2 (3% of African pop., 63% of European pop., 82% of Goan pop., 75% of Indian pop., 66% of Pakistani pop.)
Upper Volta	4.5	1.9	2
Zambia	2.6	2.5	19 (1958; 17% of African pop., 77% of European pop.)
Zanzibar	0.3	1.3	25 (towns of 5,000 or more)

Regional Comparison of World Population, 1961

Area	Total Mill.	Rate of Growth	Density
Developed Areas[1]	470	1.2	91[2]
United States	180	1.6	60
Less Developed Areas	1,509	2.4	122
Africa (incl. So. Afr.)[3]	259.2	2.2	23
Africa (excl. So. Afr.)[3]	242.5	2.2	22
Far East (incl. Japan)	343.1	2.2	210
Far East (excl. Japan)	248.2	2.6	170
19 Latin American Repubs.	209.2	2.8	27
Near East	115.2	2.6	50
South Asia	583.1	2.3	300

[1] Western Europe (excluding Greece, Portugal, Spain, Turkey and Yugoslavia), Australia, Canada, Japan, New Zealand, Republic of South Africa, and United States.

[2] Includes all Europe except European U.S.S.R.

[3] Excluding Egypt.

Sources: Agency for International Development, Statistics and Reports Division, Selected Economic Data for the Less Developed Countries (May 1963).

United Nations. Demographic Yearbook. 1962.

Regional Comparison
of Daily per Capita Caloric Intake

Developed Areas	2,950
United States	3,220
Less Developed Areas	2,240
Africa (incl. S.A.)	2,470
Africa (excl. S.A.)	2,460
Far East (excl. Japan)	2,160
19 Latin American Repubs.	2,630
Near East	2,360
South Asia	2,050

Source: **Agency** for International Development, *Selected Economic Data for the Less Developed Countries* (May 1963).

Regional Comparison
of Number of People per Physician

Developed Areas	850
United States	740
Less Developed Areas	4,400
Africa (incl. S.A.)	13,500
Africa (excl. S.A.)	22,500
Far East (incl. Japan)	2,300
Far East (excl. Japan)	5,700
19 Latin American Repubs.	1,900
Near East	2,350
South Asia	5,900

Source: **Agency** for International Development, *Selected Economic Data for the Less Developed Countries* (May 1963).

¹Ranges from 92,000 for Ethiopia to 2,000 for South Africa.

Regional Comparison of Literacy

Developed Areas	96%
United States	98%
Less Developed Areas	35%

Far East (incl. Japan)	70%
Far East (excl. Japan)	65%
Latin America	55%
Near East	30%
South Asia	25%
Africa (incl. S.A.)	17%
Africa (excl. S.A.)	15%

Source: Agency for International Development, *Selected Economic Data for the Less Developed Countries* (May 1963).

Educational Facilities in Selected African Countries

Notes (1) Although all possible care has been taken to ensure uniformity of statistics, caution should be exercised in making comparisons because of certain inevitable variations in recording data.

(2) Primary — includes elementary and primary schools providing the basic training and education to children within compulsory or customary ages of full-time education.

(3) Secondary — includes middle, secondary, and high schools.

(4) Vocational-Technical — includes secondary vocational education which aims to prepare the pupils directly for a certain trade or profession.

(5) Teacher Training — refers to secondary teacher-training (post-primary) only; higher teacher training (post-secondary) is shown with Higher.

(6) Higher — includes post-secondary teacher-training.

(7) Public schools only.

(8) Vocational schools and departments only.

(9) African education only.

(10) Number of classes or courses.

(11) Including teacher training.

(12) Including higher teacher training.

(13) Including pre-school education.

Source: Adapted from United Nations Statistical Yearbook, 1963. New York 1964.

Educational Facilities in Selected African Countries[1]

Country	Year	Primary[2]	Secondary[3]	Vocational-Technical[4]	Teacher Training[5]	Higher[6]
Algeria	1961	3,695[7]	338	25[8]	18	3
Angola	1960	2,042	46	33	2	
Basutoland[9]	1961	1,073	20	24[10]	7	1
Bechuanaland[9]	1961	229	5	1	1	
Burundi	1961	1,250	7	19	14	2
Cameroon	1961	n.a.	54	69	27	1
Cape Verde Islands	1960	147	3	6		
Central African Republic	1960	380	11	6	10	
Chad	1961	354	6	6	2	
Congo (Brazzaville)	1960	614	22	9	3	1
Congo (Leopoldville)	1961	15,970 (1959)	143	31	120	4
Dahomey	1961	587	22	154	3	
French Somaliland	1961	20	3[11]	8	3	
Gabon	1961	511	21	4	3	1
Gambia	1961	57	11	2	4	
Ghana	1959	3,713	1,463	2	1	
Guinea	1961	1,113	26	38	30	2
Ifni	1961	2	1	10	4	
Ivory Coast	1959	1,543	37	1	10	1
Kenya	1961	5,725	104	25	45[12]	1
Liberia	1961	580	33	1	4	3
Libya	1959	495	73	8	8	1
Madagascar	1960	2,605	197	6	8	1

Country	Year					(complementary courses)
Malawi[9]	1961	3,120	25	24	24	
Mali	1959	317	3	4	1	1
Mauritania	1961	228	7	85	1	
Mauritius	1961	295	92	1	6	
Mozambique	1960	3,173	23	30	4	
Niger	1961	362	8	2	260	
Nigeria	1961	15,993	983	21	1	2
Portuguese Guinea	1961	207				
Réunion	1960	347[7,13]	4	n.a.	16	
Rwanda	1961	n.a.	11	5	7	
Sao Tome and Principe	1961	23	2			
Senegal	1960	565 (1959)	34	11	n.a.	1
Seychelles	1961	30	8			1
Sierra Leone	1961	658	38			1
Somalia	1960	259	8	68	2	49
South Africa	1960	12,136	35[9]	19[9]	47[9]	3`
Southern Rhodesia	1961	2,845[9]	1	1	1	
Spanish Equatorial Africa	1960	158				
Spanish Sahara	1961	23[13]				
Sudan	1961	2,452	391	25	7	16
Swaziland	1961	305	24	3	3	
Tanganyika	1961	3,366	94	23	23	1
Togo	1961	643	31	21	2	
Tunisia	1961	1,316	n.a.	31	2	
Uganda	1960	5,968	298	95	41[12]	3
U.A.R. (Egypt)	1961	7,467	1,164	231	58	1
Upper Volta	1960	384	6	7	5	
Zambia[9]	1961	2,084	33	32	12	97
Zanzibar	1961	76	10	4	2	

Percent of African Children of School Age Attending School, According to National Income Levels*

GROUP #1

Ghana
Senegal
Liberia
Ivory Coast
Gabon

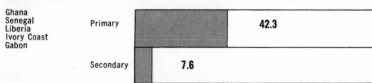

Primary — 42.3

Secondary — 7.6

GROUP #2

Kenya
Cameroon
Sudan
Madagascar
Nigeria
Congo (Leo.)

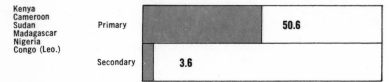

Primary — 50.6

Secondary — 3.6

GROUP #3

Togo
Uganda
Sierra Leone
Tanganyika
Mali
Guinea

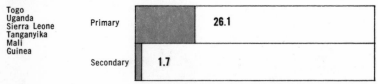

Primary — 26.1

Secondary — 1.7

GROUP #4

Congo (Braz.)
Dahomey
Niger
Chad
Upper Volta
Ethiopia
Central African
  Republic

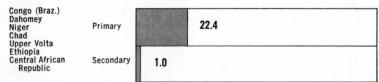

Primary — 22.4

Secondary — 1.0

National

per capita income:

Group #1 — $151-200
Group #2 — $ 71-100
Group #3 — $ 51-70
Group #4 — less than $50

Source: Adapted from *Final Report*, Conference of African States on the Development of Education in Africa, Addis Ababa, 15-25 May 1961. United Nations Economic Commission for Africa, United Nations Educational, Scientific and Cultural Organization. Unesco/ED/181.

Daily Newspaper Circulation In Selected African Countries[1]

Country	Year	Number	Circulation Total — in thousands	Circulation Per 1,000 Inhabitants
Algeria	1961	8	278	24
Angola	1961	4	44([2])	9([2])
Cameroon	1961	2	10	2
Central African Republic	1960	1	.5	.4
Chad	1961	1	.7	.3
Congo (Brazzaville)	1960	3	1.1	1
Dahomey	1961	2	3	1
Ethiopia	1960	9	42([3])	2([3])
Ghana	1961	4	224	32
Ivory Coast	1961	1	10	3
Kenya	1961	6	103	14
Liberia	1962	1	2	1.5
Libya	1961	2	8.5	7
Madagascar	1962	12	53	9
Mali	19	3([7])	.7	.2
Mauritius	1962	11	58	83
Morocco	1961	12	262([5])	22([5])
Mozambique	1960	4	21	3
Niger	1960	1	1	.3
Nigeria	1961	23	289([6])	8([6])
Portuguese Guinea	1960	1	1	2
Reunion	1960	3	22	65
Senegal	1960	1	20	6
Sierra Leone	1962	2	18	7
South-West Africa	1960	2	7.4	14
Spanish Equatorial Africa	1961	1	1	5
Sudan	1961	7	50	4
Tanganyika	1961	3	35	4
Togo	1961	1	6	4
Tunisia	1961	4	80	19
Uganda	1960	5	53	8
Zanzibar	1962	4	1.5	5

NOTES:

([1]) Publications containing general news and appearing at least 4 times per week.
([2]) Circulation figures refer to 3 dailies only.
([3]) Circulation figures refer to 6 dailies only.
([4]) Circulation figures refer to 2 dailies only.
([5]) Circulation figures refer to 11 dailies only.
([6]) Circulation figures refer to 20 dailies only.
([7]) Roneotyped bulletins.

Source: Adapted from United Nations Statistical Yearbook 1963. New York, 1964.

III. Land and Resources

A Summary Note

Much of the hope for Africa's future lies in the potential development of her resources. Her varied soil and natural vegetation lend themselves to manifold uses if creatively developed. Although many African countries are small and agricultural land is scarce, improved techniques could greatly increase agricultural production and mineral exploitation. At present, Africa, with a population 15% greater than that of the United States, produces only about 3% of the U.S. total.

The need for government initiative to stimulate growth in the early stages of economic development is generally accepted. In most cases government action is combined with private initiative in an over-all national development plan. Often, the priorities and quantities of funds allocated depend on the political orientation of individual governments. Ghana, for example, feels that considerable state intervention is both necessary and desirable, while the Ivory Coast relies very heavily on private capital for the development of its industry.

The most pressing economic need in the newly independent African countries is a modern infrastructure. This would suggest a high priority on transportation and communications since an absence of such networks inhibits the flow of goods and people and the dissemination of ideas, all of which are vital to the creation of an integrated nation and a modern economy.

Two indices of economic development are the production of energy and building materials. Many new nations of Africa rely on hydro-electric power which, although involving high initial outlays, provides a cheap source of energy over the long run. However, projects of this nature tend to be valued as prestige symbols, leading to an unnecessary duplication of installations.

An even more vital element of all development programs involves a country's most valuable natural resource — its people. Africa's labor force must be trained to perform the skilled jobs created by economic development. Africa's leaders correctly consider expanded education and health facilities as being among the most imperative of national goals.

A notable impediment to African economic development is the unfavorable trade pattern which lingers on from colonial days. Characteristically, less developed regions export unfinished primary products and import manufactured goods. In the case of Africa, this imbalance is compounded by reliance on a single crop for a major part of individual countries' cash incomes. This subjects African countries to world market price fluctuations which are quite beyond their control. At present, Africa's share in world trade is only about 3%.

A particularly weak link in the commercial cycle is intra-African trade itself. This, too, is a carry-over from the colonial division of Africa into separate spheres of influence and the consequent orientation of the colonies' trade to their respective mother countries. At present, intra-African trade amounts to $1.50 per capita and, if trade between South Africa and Southern Rhodesia is excluded, the sum drops to $0.50 per capita. The establishment of new intra-African trade patterns and the development of complementary economies will have inevitable implications for the whole sphere of intra-African relations.

Even with increased and more efficient production and improved trade relations, Africa's resources still remain grossly inferior to her needs. For many years to come most African countries will rely on outside assistance, both multilateral and bilateral, to fill the gap. Multilateral assistance has become increasingly important in recent years. Newly independent countries have less fear of alienating a portion of their sovereignty through external commitments by dealing with the United Nations and its related agencies. Africa's share of the net assistance extended by all major multilateral organizations to less developed countries amounted to 52% in 1960 and 40% in 1961. The detailed list of Special Fund Projects illustrates the variety of undertakings sponsored by multilateral assistance agencies in Africa.

At the same time, bilateral assistance has increased markedly. United States Government assistance doubled from $258 million in 1951/60 to $515 million in 1961/2. The greatest share of this rise was aid to newly independent countries, which jumped from $5 million to $41 million during this period. The purpose of U.S. aid is to further stability and development of the basic infrastructure, both of which are preconditions of pervasive economic development.

Communist aid, on the other hand, is often channeled to carefully selected high impact projects and is designed to create a climate conducive to the spread of Communist ideas and influence. Thus, in 1961 Ghana, Somalia, and Mali were the largest beneficiaries. Together with the East European Communist states, the Soviet Union offers an alternative source of aid and avenue of trade which releases the African countries from their dependence on the West. Communist China, for its part, seeks to further its own cause by capitalizing on its non-European status and by suggesting that it can best serve as an example for developing countries. The form of aid most frequently employed by the Communist states takes the form of low-interest credits which allows the donor to exert a certain amount of control over the domestic and foreign economic policies of the recipient. Communist China occasionally makes outright grants. As with United States aid, technical experts generally are a part of aid given for specific projects.

A variety of Communist initiatives notwithstanding and despite some formal protestations most former colonies welcome aid from those European powers which had formerly ruled or administered them, especially if it is channelled through multi-national organizations such as the European Development Fund. Hence, for the foreseeable future, there is likely to be a complicated interplay of international forces in the field of economic aid and technical assistance.

Principal Vegetation Regions of Africa

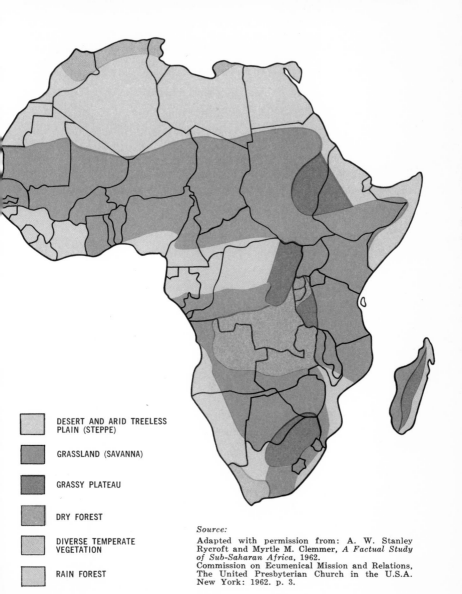

DESERT AND ARID TREELESS
PLAIN (STEPPE)

GRASSLAND (SAVANNA)

GRASSY PLATEAU

DRY FOREST

DIVERSE TEMPERATE
VEGETATION

RAIN FOREST

Source:
Adapted with permission from: A. W. Stanley
Rycroft and Myrtle M. Clemmer, *A Factual Study
of Sub-Saharan Africa*, 1962.
Commission on Ecumenical Mission and Relations,
The United Presbyterian Church in the U.S.A.
New York: 1962. p. 3.

Total Land Area and Agricultural Land in Africa

Country	Total 1,000 sq. mi.	Similar in Size to: (U.S. State)	Agricultural Land % of total area	acres per capita
Algeria	920	Oklahoma+Texas+Alaska	19	10
Angola	481	Texas+New Mexico+Oregon	24	15
Basutoland	12	Maryland+Delaware	94	10
Bechuanaland	275	Washington+Oregon+Idaho+Maine	58	283
Burundi	11	Maryland+Rhode Island	n.a.	n.a.
Cameroon	183	Minnesota+Colorado	35	10
Central African Republic	238	Arizona+New Mexico	n.a.	n.a.
Chad	496	Texas+New Mexico+Arizona	47	49
Congo (Braz.)	132	Minnesota+Wisconsin	n.a.	n.a.
Congo (Leo.)	906	U.S. East of Mississippi	22	9
Dahomey	45	Pennsylvania	n.a.	n.a.
Ethiopia	457	Texas+California+Indiana	60	9
Gabon	103	Colorado	n.a.	n.a.
Gambia	4	Connecticut	21	2
Ghana	92	Oregon	22	2
Guinea	95	Oregon	n.a.	n.a.
Ivory Coast	125	New Mexico+Connecticut	n.a.	n.a.
Kenya	225	Colorado+New Mexico	28	2
Liberia	43	Tennessee	20	6
Libya	679	Alaska+Oregon	6	22
Madagascar	228	Colorado+New Mexico	65	16
Malawi	45	Pennsylvania	30	3
Mali	465	Texas+California+Mississippi	n.a.	n.a.
Mauritania	419	Texas+California	n.a.	n.a.
Mauritius	1	Rhode Island	69	1

Country	Total 1,000 sq. mi.	Similar in Size to: (U.S. State)	Agricultural Land % of total area	acres per capita
Morocco	171	Illinois+Indiana+Ohio+Kentucky	40	3
Mozambique	298	Minnesota+North Dakota+ South Dakota+Nebraska	60	17
Niger	459	Texas+New Mexico+ Oklahoma+Hawaii	25	23
Nigeria	357	North Dakota+South Dakota+ Nebraska+Minnesota+Iowa	23	2
Rwanda	10	Maryland	n.a.	n.a.
Senegal	76	Nebraska	40	6
Sierra Leone	28	Maine	81	6
Somalia	246	Washington+Oregon+Idaho	34	26
South Africa	472	Texas+California+Florida	83	14
South-West Africa	318	Oregon+Washington+California	n.a.	n.a.
Southern Rhodesia	140	Montana	17	4
Sudan	967	U.S. East of Mississippi+ Missouri	12	6
Swaziland	7	New Jersey	94	15
Tanganyika	362	Texas+Colorado	19	4
Togo	22	West Virginia	41	4
Tunisia	48	New York	40	3
U.A.R. (Egypt)	386	Texas+New Mexico	3	0.2
Uganda	94	Oregon	12	1
Upper Volta	106	Colorado	n.a.	n.a.
Zambia	288	Alabama+Georgia+Mississippi+ N. Car.+S. Car.+Arkansas	41	29
Zanzibar	1	Rhode Island	59	1

Source: Area and agricultural land from Agency for International Development, Statistics and Reports Division. *Selected Economic Data for the Less Developed Countries.* May 1963.

Government

Capital

Expenditure

in

Development

Programs

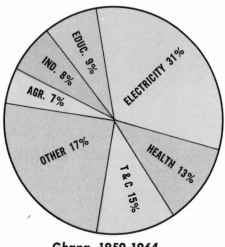

Ghana 1959-1964

Sources:

United Nations. *Economic Bulletin for Africa,* Vol. II, No. 2, June 1962, and individual development plans.

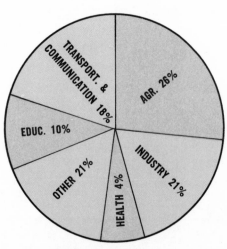

Guinea 1960-1963

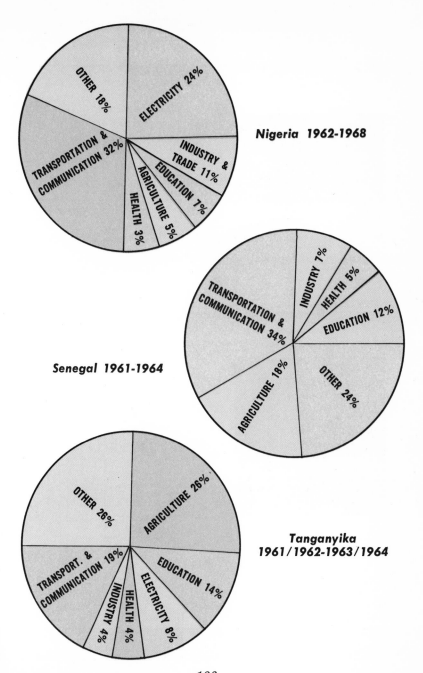

Nigeria 1962-1968

ELECTRICITY 24%

OTHER 18%

INDUSTRY & TRADE 11%

TRANSPORTATION & COMMUNICATION 32%

EDUCATION 7%

AGRICULTURE 5%

HEALTH 3%

Senegal 1961-1964

TRANSPORTATION & COMMUNICATION 34%

INDUSTRY 7%

HEALTH 5%

EDUCATION 12%

AGRICULTURE 18%

OTHER 24%

Tanganyika
1961/1962-1963/1964

OTHER 26%

AGRICULTURE 26%

TRANSPORT. & COMMUNICATION 19%

EDUCATION 14%

INDUSTRY 4%

HEALTH 4%

ELECTRICITY 8%

123

$3,000

United States — $2,820

Regional Comparison of Gross National Product Per Capita

(each coin represents $50.)

$2,500

$2,000

Developed Areas — $1,630

$1,500

SOURCE:

Selected Economic Data for the Less Developed Countries, Agency for International Development, May 1963.

(1) Africa:
    including S.A.—$120.
    excluding S.A.—$100.
(2) Far East:
    includ. Japan—$210.
    exclud. Japan—$95.

$1,000

$500

L. A. — $265
Near East — $205

Less Developed Areas — $125

Africa(1) — $100
Far East(2) — $95
South Asia — $80

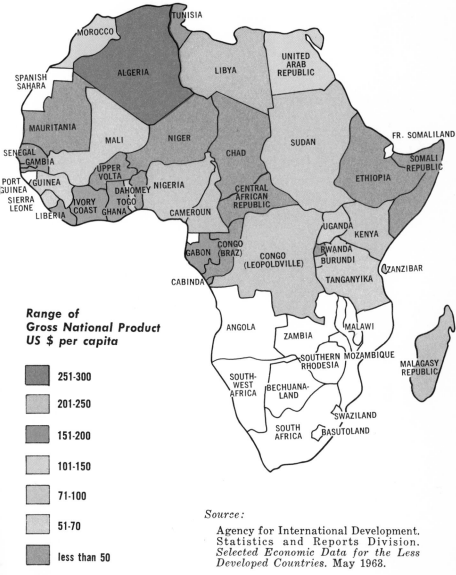

Approximate Level of Gross National Product Per Capita in Selected African Countries (1961)

TUNISIA
MOROCCO
SPANISH SAHARA
ALGERIA
LIBYA
UNITED ARAB REPUBLIC
MAURITANIA
MALI
NIGER
SUDAN
FR. SOMALILAND
SENEGAL
GAMBIA
PORT. GUINEA
GUINEA
UPPER VOLTA
CHAD
SOMALI REPUBLIC
SIERRA LEONE
DAHOMEY
NIGERIA
ETHIOPIA
LIBERIA
IVORY COAST
TOGO
GHANA
CAMEROUN
CENTRAL AFRICAN REPUBLIC
UGANDA
KENYA
GABON
CONGO (BRAZ)
CONGO (LEOPOLDVILLE)
RWANDA
BURUNDI
ZANZIBAR
CABINDA
TANGANYIKA
ANGOLA
ZAMBIA
MALAWI
MOZAMBIQUE
SOUTHERN RHODESIA
MALAGASY REPUBLIC
SOUTH-WEST AFRICA
BECHUANA-LAND
SWAZILAND
SOUTH AFRICA
BASUTOLAND

Range of Gross National Product US $ per capita

251-300

201-250

151-200

101-150

71-100

51-70

less than 50

Source:

Agency for International Development. Statistics and Reports Division. *Selected Economic Data for the Less Developed Countries.* May 1963.

125

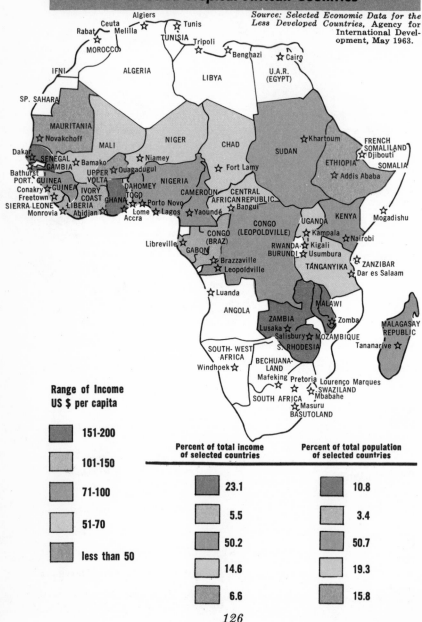

Approximate Level of Per Capita National Income In Selected Tropical African Countries

Source: Selected Economic Data for the Less Developed Countries, Agency for International Development, May 1963.

Range of Income US $ per capita

- 151-200
- 101-150
- 71-100
- 51-70
- less than 50

Percent of total income of selected countries	Percent of total population of selected countries
23.1	10.8
5.5	3.4
50.2	50.7
14.6	19.3
6.6	15.8

The Movement of Labor: Employment in Non-Agricultural Activities In Selected African Countries[1]

Index: 1958 = 100

Country	1955	1956	1957	1959[2]	1960	1961	1962
Cameroon	102	104	100	95	91	94	72
Gabon	n.a.	90	114	112	112	112	129
Ghana	82	91	95	106	111	122	n.a.
Kenya	107	105	105	100	102	98	98
Nigeria	n.a.	95	100	99	106	82	n.a.
N. Rhodesia	91	99	103	95	93	89	86
Sierra Leone [3]	87	100	103	100	97	111	n.a.
South Africa [4]	93	96	100	101	101	102	103
S. Rhodesia	85	92	98	100	100	97	94
Tanganyika [5]	97	104	101	96	94	98	94
Uganda	94	93	99	99	99	98	94
U.A.R. (Egypt)	n.a.	n.a.	n.a.	97	94	98	n.a.
Nyasaland	89	96	99	97	93	91	84

[1] One of the prerequisites of a developing economy is the gradual shift of the labor force from subsistence agriculture to industry. As this table shows, some African countries actually exhibit a reverse trend.

[2] Figures include wage earners and salaried employees in mining, manufacturing, construction, transport, commerce, personal and public services. Employment in agriculture, forestry and fishing are excluded.

[3] Excluding manufacturing.

[4] Excluding services, public utilities, commerce.

[5] Prior to 1958, Africans only.

Source: United Nations Statistical Yearbook 1963. New York, 1964.

127

Regional Comparison of Commercial and Passenger Vehicles In Use

WORLD[1]

128.8 MILLION

AFRICA
2.7 MILLION

SOUTH AMERICA
3.1 MILLION

OCEANIA
3.6 MILLION

ASIA[3]
4.5 MILLION

EUROPE[2]
31.8 MILLION

NORTH AMERICA
73.1 MILLION

[1] Excluding Albania, Bulgaria, Communist China, Czechoslovakia, Eastern Germany, Hungary, North Korea, North Viet-Nam, Romania, USSR.

[2] Excluding European countries as above.

[3] Excluding Asiatic countries as above.

Source: United Nations Statistical Yearbook 1962.

Miles of Railroad Tracks
In Selected African Countries

Each Box = 1,000 Miles of Track

Country	Miles
South Africa	13,580
Kenya, Uganda, Tanganyika	3,465
Congo (Leo.)	3,125
United Arab Republic	2,962
Zambia-Malawi	2,905
Sudan	2,560
Algeria	2,545
Angola	1,802
Nigeria	1,790
Mozambique	1,671
Tunisia	1,220
Morocco	1,086

Source: Adapted from: *Universal Directory of Railway Officials and Railway Year Book,* London, 1961-62. The Directory Publishing Co.. Ltd.

Production of Cement of Selected
African Countries — 1962

Country	Thousand Metric Tons
Angola	169
Ethiopia	41
Kenya	334
Morocco	700
Mozambique	179
Nigeria	479
Senegal	183
South Africa	2658
Tunisia	363
Uganda	56
United Arab Republic (Egypt)	2289

Source: United Nations Statistical Yearbook 1963. New York, 1964.

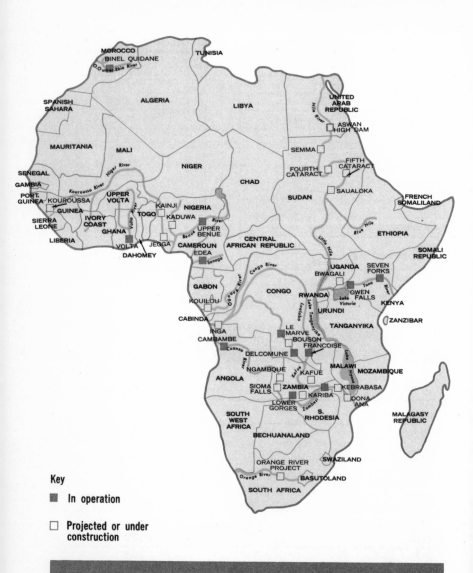

Key

■ In operation

□ Projected or under
construction

Site of Existing and Planned Hydroelectric
Power Projects of 100 MW or More

Production of Electricity of Selected African Countries — 1962

Country	Million KWH
Algeria	1,154
Angola	1,837 ('61)
Central African Republic	12.1
Chad	11
Congo (Brazzaville)	36.6
Gabon	27.1
Ghana	431
Ivory Coast	120.2
Kenya	239
Madagascar	119.6
Mauritius	77
Morocco	1,097
Niger	12.7
Nigeria	786
N. Rhodesia	1,926
Nyasaland	38.3
South Africa	26,105
South West Africa	210
Southern Rhodesia	1,694
Tanganyika	179.2
Togo	7.7
Uganda	433.1
Upper Volta	13.5
Zanzibar	13.4

Source: United Nations Statistical Yearbook 1963. New York, 1964.

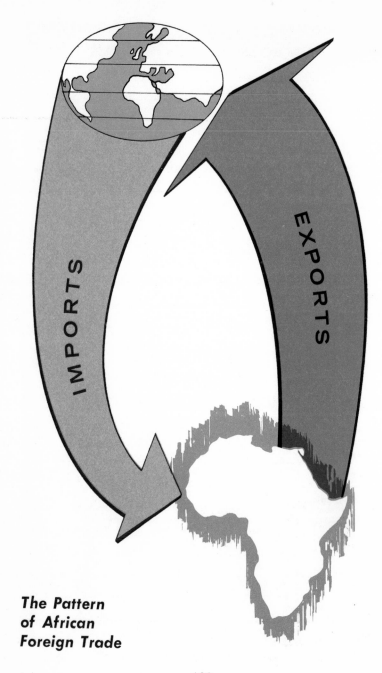

IMPORTS

EXPORTS

**The Pattern
of African
Foreign Trade**

IMPORTS	EXPORTS
HEAVY MACHINERY	BANANAS
MOTOR VEHICLES AND PARTS	SUGAR
FUEL	TEA
CEMENT	MAIZE
LUMBER	DRIED FISH
STEEL	RAW COTTON
IRON	TOBACCO
MEDICAL	SISAL
APPLIANCES	PALM KERNELS
DRUGS	NUTS AND OIL
CHEMICALS	RICE
SOAP	SPICES
BEER	OLIVE OIL
ELECTRICAL EQUIPMENT	RUBBER
CIGARETTES	TIMBER
FOODSTUFFS	CATTLE, HIDES AND MEAT
WAXES	TUSKS
PAINTS	COPPER
VARNISHES	BAUXITE
WINE	MANGANESE
SUGAR	DIAMONDS
COTTON GOODS	GOLD
THREAD	IRON ORE
SHOES	TIN
COFFEE	PHOSPHATES
COCOA	COTTON
PEANUTS	

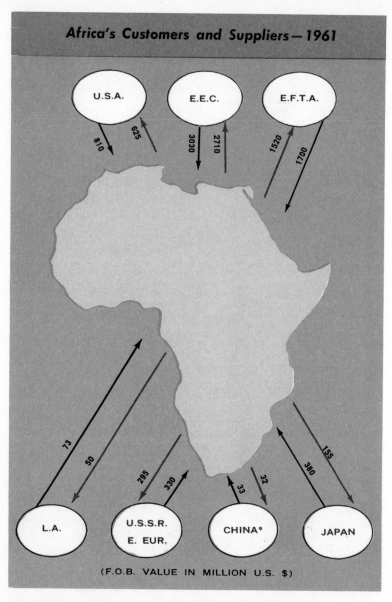

Africa's Customers and Suppliers—1961

(F.O.B. VALUE IN MILLION U.S. $)

Source: United Nations. Yearbook of International Trade Statistics 1961.
New York, 1963.

*Mainland China plus N. Korea, N. Viet-Nam, Mongolia.

Africa's Share of World Trade

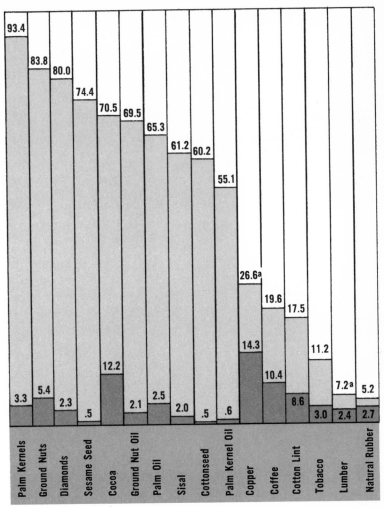

Share of selected items in total tropical African exports

Africa's exports of these items as a share of total world exports

Palm Kernels	93.4 / 3.3
Ground Nuts	83.8 / 5.4
Diamonds	80.0 / 2.3
Sesame Seed	74.4 / .5
Cocoa	70.5 / 12.2
Ground Nut Oil	69.5 / 2.1
Palm Oil	65.3 / 2.5
Sisal	61.2 / 2.0
Cottonseed	60.2 / .5
Palm Kernel Oil	55.1 / .6
Copper	26.6[a] / 14.3
Coffee	19.6 / 10.4
Cotton Lint	17.5 / 8.6
Tobacco	11.2 / 3.0
Lumber	7.2[a] / 2.4
Natural Rubber	5.2 / 2.7

(a) By quantity, not value.

Source:
Adapted from FAO Africa Survey:
Report on the Possibilities of African Rural Development in Relation to Economic and Social Growth. Rome, 1962.

Principal Exports of Selected African Countries

Country	Product	Percent of Each Country's 1961 Exports	%
Algeria	petroleum		45%
Angola	coffee		36%
Basutoland	wool-mohair		72%
Bechuanaland	cattle & prods.		75%
Burundi	coffee		75%
Cameroon	cocoa/ coffee		44%
Central African Republc	cotton/ coffee		71%
Chad	cotton		81%
Congo (B)	wood & prods.		60%
Congo (L)	copper		34%
Dahomey	palm products		54%
Ethiopia	coffee		56%
Gabon	wood & prods.		71%
Gambia	peanuts		91%
Ghana	cocoa		58%
Guinea	alumina		48%
Ivory Coast	coffee/ cocoa		67%
Kenya	coffee		19%
Liberia	rubber/ iron ore		89%
Libya	petroleum		55%
Malagasy	coffee		28%
Malawi	tea		n.a.

Principal Exports of Selected African Countries

Country	Product	Percent of Each Country's 1961 Exports	%
Mali	livestock		31%
Mauritania	livestock		n.a.
Mauritius	sugar		90%
Morocco	phosphates		22%
Mozambique	cotton		27%
Niger	peanuts		75%
Nigeria	palm products		19%
Rwanda	coffee/ mins.		85%
Senegal			83%
Sierra Leone	diamonds		55%
Somali	banannas		50%
S. Africa	gold		38%
S. Rhodesia	tobacco		n.a.
Sudan	cotton		50%
Swaziland	asbestos		45%
Tanganyika	sisal		27%
Togo	cocoa/ coffee		55%
Tunisia	wine		14.4% (1960)
U.A.R. (Egypt)	cotton		66%
Uganda	cotton		35%
Upper Volta	livestock		60%
Zambia	copper		90%
Zanzibar	cloves & oil		58%

Source:
Agency for International Development. Statistics and Reports Division.
Selected Economic Data for the Less Developed Countries. May 1963.

Intra-African Trade of Selected West African Countries
1961

IMPORTING COUNTRIES

Tons	Ivory Coast	Dahomey	Upper Volta	Niger	Mali	Mauritania	Senegal	Total
Ivory Coast		3534	4710	1472	15,413	29	46,781	71,939
Dahomey	2330		12	930	47	4	1261	4584
Upper Volta	377	948		24	888	—	791	3028
Niger	10	1476	125		4947	—	654	7212
Mali	18,136	1	2728	865		88	1	21,819
Mauritania	28	—	—	—	353		1871	2252
Senegal	77,726	6287	2984	5366	244	25,029		117,636
Total	98,607	12,246	10,559	8,657	21,892	25,150	51,359	228,470

EXPORTING COUNTRIES

Source:
Notes d'Information et Statistiques.
Banque Centrale des Etats de l'Afrique de l'Ouest, no. 93, April 1963.

138

United Nations Technical Assistance To Africa[1]
1961-1963

ALGERIA	$1,251,100		MAURITANIA	$637,000
BASUTOLAND	$268,640		MAURITIUS	$294,410
BECHUANALAND	$137,106		MOROCCO	$7,816,298
BURUNDI	$834,500		NIGER	$1,098,800
CAMEROON[2]	$2,682,100		NIGERIA	$14,363,445
CENTRAL AFRICAN REPUBLIC	$801,570		PORTUGUESE AFRICAN TERRITORIES	$31,200
CHAD	$875,927		RHODESIA AND NYASALAND	$2,905,600
CONGO (BRAZZAVILLE)	$2,418,420		RWANDA	$843,500
CONGO (LEOPOLDVILLE)	$1,416,700		SENEGAL	$5,120,829
DAHOMEY	$874,200		SIERRA LEONE	$891,574
ETHIOPIA	$3,455,447		SOMALIA	$4,062,068
FRENCH SOMALILAND	$50,400		SUDAN	$8,828,892
GABON	$2,846,800		SWAZILAND	$143,826
GAMBIA	$240,195		TANGANYIKA	$1,943,400
GHANA	$5,872,048		TOGO	$3,314,823
GUINEA	$2,968,512		TUNISIA	$6,479,930
IVORY COAST	$2,096,100		UGANDA	$2,104,100
KENYA	$4,169,200		UNITED ARAB REPUBLIC	$93,660,345
LIBERIA	$1,879,310		UPPER VOLTA	$3,296,750
LIBYA	$3,978,278		ZANZIBAR	$274,600
MADAGASCAR	$3,795,250			
MALI	$3,055,100			

[1]Includes only Expanded Technical Assistance Program (EPTA) and Special Fund,
[2]Including Southern Cameroon.

Source: Department of State, Office of International Affairs.

I Projects of the United Nations Special Fund in Africa

PROJECT	Executing Agency[1]	Date Approved	Duration	Cost US $
CAMEROON				
1. Secondary School Teacher Training Institute, Yaounde	UNESCO	5/61	6 yrs	2,692,800
CONGO (BRAZZAVILLE)				
1. Secondary School Teacher Training Institute, Brazzaville . . .	UNESCO	1/62	6 yrs	2,960,200
2. Survey of the Water Resources of the Niari Valley	FAO	5/62	3 yrs	778,700
ETHIOPIA				
1. Survey of the Awash River Basin	FAO	5/60	3 yrs	1,257,100
2. School for Animal Health Assistants	FAO	12/60	5 yrs	722,700
GABON				
1. Iron Ore Transport Survey . .	IBRD	1/63	2 yrs	2,892,000
GHANA				
1. Survey of the Volta Flood Plain	FAO	5/59	3 yrs	540,000
2. Institute of Public Administration, Accra	UN	5/61	5 yrs	1,845,700
3. Land and Water Surveys in the Upper and Northern Regions . .	FAO	1/62	3 yrs	1,181,700
4. Food Research and Development Unit	FAO	1/63	5 yrs	1,880,800
5. Preparation of a Master Plan for Water Supply and Sewage . .	WHO	1/63	2 yrs	2,153,300
GUINEA				
1. Resources Development Survey (cancelled before completion)	UN	5/59	1 yr	126,000
2. Improvement and Expansion of Rice Cultivation in the Coastal Lowlands	FAO	1/63	5 yrs	1,818,100
IVORY COAST				
1. Secondary School Teacher Training Institute, Abidjan	UNESCO	5/61	6 yrs	3,150,400

PROJECT	Executing Agency[1]	Date Approved	Duration	Cost US $
LIBERIA				
1. Agricultural Training and Research	FAO	12/60	6 yrs	1,756,900
LIBYA				
1. College of Advanced Technology	UNESCO	12/59	6 yrs	3,063,950
2. Institute of Radio and Tele-communications	ITU	12/60	5 yrs	1,183,600
MALAGASY				
1. Educational Training and Research Institute, Tananarive . .	UNESCO	1/63	6 yrs	2,924,200
MALI				
1. Secondary School Teacher Training Institute, Bamako	UNESCO	1/62	6 yrs	3,688,900
2. Improvement and Expansion of Rice Cultivation	FAO	5/62	5 yrs	1,463,000
MOROCCO				
1. Engineering School	UNESCO	5/60	5 yrs	2,751,500
2. Rural Economic Pre-Investment Project for the Western Rif . .	FAO	5/60	2 yrs	1,882,800
3. Training Center for Civil Aviation and Meteorology	ICAO	12/60	5 yrs	1,772,200
4. Institute for Instructor Training for Leather and Textile Workers .	ILO	1/62	4 yrs	2,472,800
5. Secondary School Teacher Training Institute, Rabat	UNESCO	5/62	5 yrs	2,743,900
6. Integrated Economic Plan for Agricultural Development of the Sebou Region	FAO	1/63	3 yrs	4,449,000
NIGERIA				
1. Niger Dams Survey	IBRD	12/59	1 yr	2,425,000
2. Federal Higher Teacher Training College	UNESCO	12/60	5 yrs	2,852,200
3. Soil and Water Resources Survey of the Sokoto Valley . .	FAO	5/61	4 yrs	2,272,300
4. National Training Scheme for Vocational Instructors and Foremen	ILO	5/61	4 yrs	1,507,500

PROJECT	Executing Agency[1]	Date Approved	Duration	Cost US $
NIGERIA (Contd.)				
5. Fisheries Survey in the Western Region	FAO	5/61	4 yrs	829,000
6. Secondary School Teacher Training College, Northern Region . .	UNESCO	1/62	5 yrs	3,730,200
7. Forestry Department, University College, Ibadan	FAO	5/62	6 yrs	1,551,800
8. Secondary School Teacher Training College, Eastern Region . .	UNESCO	5/62	5 yrs	3,688,500
9. Secondary School Teacher Training College, Western Region . .	UNESCO	1/63	5 yrs	3,583,700
10. Federal Civil Aviation Training Center, Kaduna	ICAO	1/63	5 yrs	3,698,000
SENEGAL				
1. Instructor and Foreman Training Center	ILO	5/61	4 yrs	1,625,500
2. Secondary School Teacher Training Institute, Dakar	UNESCO	1/62	6 yrs	3,179,700
3. Rural Vocational Training Program	ILO	1/62	4 yrs	2,680,200
4. Mineral Survey	UN	1/63	3 yrs	1,520,600
SOMALIA				
1. Agricultural and Water Survey	FAO	12/60	4 yrs	1,218,800
2. Mineral and Groundwater Survey	UN	1/62	4 yrs	874,300
SUDAN				
1. Animal Health Institute . . .	FAO	1/60	5 yrs	459,900
2. Hides, Skins and Leather: Development and Training Project . .	FAO	12/60	4 yrs	868,600
3. Forestry Research and Education Center, Khartoum	FAO	5/61	5 yrs	1,222,600
4. Land and Water Use Survey of Kordofan Province	FAO	5/61	4 yrs	1,389,900
5. Training Institute for Secondary School Teachers	UNESCO	5/61	5 yrs	3,015,400
6. Post and Telegraph Training Center at Khartoum	ITU	1/62	5 yrs	1,936,900
7. Electric Power Survey . . .	IBRD	5/62	1 yr	141,200
8. Land and Water Resources Survey in the Jebel Marra Area . . .	FAO	5/62	4 yrs	3,056,100
TOGO				
1. Soil and Water Resources Survey	FAO	5/60	3 yrs	963,000
2. Survey of Groundwater and Mineral Resources	UN	1/62	3 yrs	1,793,500

PROJECT	Executing Agency[1]	Date Approved	Duration	Cost US $
TUNISIA				
1. Agricultural Investigations and Development Planning in Central Tunisia	FAO	5/60	5 yrs	2,457,200
2. Training Center for Civil Aviation and Meteorology	ICAO	1/60	5 yrs	2,395,500
3. Research and Training on Irrigation with Saline Water . . .	UNESCO	1/62	5 yrs	1,817,800
4. National Vocational Training and Productivity Institute, Rades . .	ILO	1/62	5 yrs	2,644,700
5. Preparation of an Integrated Rural Plan for Central Tunisia .	FAO	1/63	3 yrs	2,006,600
UGANDA				
1. Aerial Geophysical Survey . .	UN	5/60	1 yr	453,500
2. Kampala Technical Institute .	UNESCO	1/62	6 yrs	5,112,500
UNITED ARAB REPUBLIC				
1. Pilot Project for Drainage of Irrigated Land	FAO	5/59	3 yrs	1,365,000
2. Soil Survey Project	FAO	5/59	4 yrs	827,500
3. Civil Aviation Training Institute	ICAO	5/60	5 yrs	1,860,500
4. Cotton Research Laboratory .	FAO	12/60	4 yrs	1,465,300
5. Animal Health Institute . . .	FAO	12/60	4 yrs	1,005,000
6. Vocational Instructor Training Institute	ILO	12/60	4 yrs	1,447,100
7. National Physical Laboratory for Meteorology	UNESCO	5/61	5 yrs	4,973,700
8. Central Agricultural Pesticides Laboratory, Cairo	FAO	5/61	4 yrs	986,000
9. Institute of Small Industries, Kubba	ILO	1/62	4 yrs	1,298,600
10. Mansoura Institute for Higher Education	UNESCO	5/62	5 yrs	4,870,400
11. Vegetable Improvement and Seed Production Research Center, Dokki	FAO	1/63	5 yrs	1,169,900

[1]*Glossary of abbreviations:*
 a. UNESCO — United Nations Educational, Scientific, and Cultural Organization.
 b. FAO — Food and Agriculture Organization.
 c. ICAO — International Civil Aviation Organization.
 d. ILO — International Labor Organization.
 e. IBRD — International Bank for Reconstruction and Development (World Bank).
 f. WHO — World Health Organization.
 g. ITU — International Telecommunication Union.

Source: Target: an expanding world economy. A United Nations Special Fund Report,. 1963.

World Bank Aid To Africa[1]

ALGERIA	$60 MILLION
CONGO (LEOPOLDVILLE)	$120 MILLION
EAST AFRICA[2]	$24 MILLION
ETHIOPIA	$41.9 MILLION
FORMER FRENCH WEST AFRICA[3]	$7.1 MILLION
GABON	$35 MILLION
GHANA	$4.7 MILLION
KENYA	$14 MILLION
MAURITANIA	$66 MILLION
MOROCCO	$16.5 MILLION
NIGERIA	$41.5 MILLION
RHODESIA AND NYASALAND	$146.6 MILLION
RWANDA AND BURUNDI	$4.8 MILLION
SOUTH AFRICA	$221.8 MILLION
SUDAN	$87 MILLION
SWAZILAND	$7 MILLION
TANGANYIKA	$2.8 MILLION
TUNISIA	$8.5 MILLION
UGANDA	$8.4 MILLION
UNITED ARAB REPUBLIC	$56.5 MILLION

[1]Includes World Bank, operating in Africa since 1950; International Finance Corporation (IFC), investing in Africa since 1960; and International Development Association (IDA), making credits in Africa since 1961.

[2]Kenya, Uganda, Tanganyika.

[3]For Railroads in Senegal, Mali, Ivory Coast, annd Upper Voita.

Source: The World Bank Group in Africa, September 1963. International Bank for Reconstruction and Development, International Finance Corporation, International Development Association.

Soviet Bloc Economic Assistance To Africa*
1959-1961

UNITED ARAB REPUBLIC	$464 MILLION
GHANA	$146 MILLION
ETHIOPIA	$127 MILLION
GUINEA	$86 MILLION
SOMALI REPUBLIC	$82 MILLION
MALI	$55 MILLION
TUNISIA	$54 MILLION
SUDAN	$37 MILLION
MOROCCO	$5 MILLION
LIBERIA	$3 MILLION

*Commitments only; no accurate data are available on actual disbursements.

Source: Economic Commission for Africa, *International Economic Assistance to Africa*, 1961. 19 February 1963.

United States Government Assistance To Selected African Countries — 1960-1962

UNITED ARAB REPUBLIC	$454.1 MILLION
MOROCCO	$213 MILLION
TUNISIA	$165 MILLION
GHANA[2]	$130 MILLION
CONGO (LEOPOLDVILLE)	$105.7 MILLION
LIBYA	$92 MILLION
LIBERIA	$45 MILLION
SUDAN	$43 MILLION
ETHIOPIA	$34.6 MILLION
NIGERIA	$29.2 MILLION
SOMALI REPUBLIC	$20.2 MILLION
GUINEA[2]	$9.4 MILLION
MALI	$3.2 MILLION
RHODESIA AND NYASALAND[3]	$23 MILLION
SOUTH AFRICA[3]	$39 MILLION

Source: Economic Commission for Africa, *International Economic Assistance to Africa, 1961,* 19 February 1963, and Agency for International Development.
[1]Through June 30, 1962.
[2]For fiscal year 1962 only.
[3]Net repayment to United States.

European Development Fund Aid To Africa as of June 1962

ALGERIA	$17.7 MILLION
CAMEROON	$34 MILLION
CENTRAL AFRICAN REPUBLIC	$10.8 MILLION
CHAD	$15.5 MILLION
CONGO (BRAZZAVILLE)	$14.6 MILLION
CONGO (LEOPOLDVILLE)	$5.0 MILLION
DAHOMEY	$10.5 MILLION
FRENCH SOMALILAND	$.74 MILLION
GABON	$9 MILLION
IVORY COAST	$25.9 MILLION
MALAGASY REPUBLIC	$28.7 MILLION
MALI	$15.1 MILLION
MAURITANIA	$9.8 MILLION
NIGER	$13 MILLION
REUNION	$1.7 MILLION
RWANDA AND BURUNDI	$6.2 MILLION
SAHARA	$2.8 MILLION
SENEGAL	$28.4 MILLION
SOMALIA	$4.8 MILLION
TOGO	$10 MILLION
UPPER VOLTA	$14.9 MILLION
OTHER AND REGIONAL	$2 MILLION

Source: Economic Commission for Africa, *International Economic Assistance to Africa, 1961,* 19 February 1963.

Bilateral Technical Assistance To Selected African Countries[1]

GUINEA

DONOR	AMOUNT	PURPOSE
W. Germany	DM50 million credits Technicians	Water-supply system and road construction.
Yugoslavia	$2.25 million $5 million Technicians	Construction of dam. Commercial credit. Doctors, teachers. Conakry city improvement plan.
Egypt	$15 million loan $16 million credit Technicians	Machinery and salaries of technicians. Cotton textile purchases. Construction and railroad engineers, teachers, pilots.
Ghana	$28 million Technicians	Loan offered at independence.
Morocco	$2 million credit Technicians	Foodstuffs and consumer goods.
Israel	Credits Grants Technicians	Teachers.
United Kingdom	Credits Grants Technicians	Teachers.
Italy	Credit Grants Technicians	5 scholarships for study in Italy.
U.S.S.R.	$56 million credits $8 million credit Amount unknown $1 million Technicians	Polytechnic institute, shortwave transmitter, modernization of port, airport runway, railway, road improvement, minerals survey, industrial projects. Imports of rails and other heavy equipment. Patrice Lumumba printing plant. 500-bed hospital in Kankan. Teachers, mining and civil engineers.
Communist China	$24 million interest-free loan Equipment Technicians	Agricultural projects, including experimental tea farm. Gift of 10 trucks, 10 projectors, 10 electrical generators, X-Ray equipment, pharmaceutical products. 150 agricultural advisors.

146

DONOR	AMOUNT	PURPOSE
Hungary	$2.4 million credit Technicians Grants	Commercial goods. Mechanics, teachers, medical personnel.
Czechoslovakia	$10 million credit Grants Technicians	Commercial goods. Assistance to Air Guinea. Tannery at Kindia. Economic advisers, doctors, teachers, airport, operating personnel and crews.
Bulgaria	$2 million credit Grants Technicians	Export of commercial goods. Water resource survey.
Poland	$5 million credit Technicians Grants	Commercial goods. Operation of 6 modern fishing trawlers; joint ownership of company. Training Guinean fishing crews; engineers, doctors, teachers.
East Germany	$5 million credit Equipment	Commercial goods. Printing plant. Outdoor theater. Loudspeakers.

TANGANYIKA

DONOR	AMOUNT	PURPOSE
United Kingdom	$23.8 million grants $11.2 million loans $8.4 million loan $16.8 million grant $16.8 million loan $3 million $.5 million grant	Development plan. Development plan. Commutation of civil servants pensions. Civil service career compensation. Civil service career compensation. Expatriate salaries. Military forces.
West Germany	$1.4 million $2.2 million $.8 million $1.8 million $1 million $1.4 million Equipment Technicians	Development company. Southern Highlands Railway. Agricultural training. Agricultural extension work. Land and water planning. Water. Business training institute; Technical college and trade school; cooperative college. Staff for above; geologists, cartographers, geotechnicians.
Israel	Scholarships Technicians Equipment	100 students trained annually. Advisers in consumer cooperatives. Farm institute.
France	Scholarships Technicians	3 or more trainees annually. Hydroelectric power feasibility studies.

SOMALI REPUBLIC

DONOR	AMOUNT	PURPOSE
Italy	$3.5 million	Budgetary aid.
	$1 million	Development program.
	$2 million	Technical assistance.
	$4.8 million loan	Banana plantations improvement; purchase of sugar refinery.
	$.5 million credits	Improve telephone system.
West Germany	$6 million loan	Textile plant; equipment for fishing industry; road construction.
	Equipment	Technical school; trucks.
	Scholarships	Training in Germany.
United Kingdom	$2.1 million	Budgetary aid.
	$2 million	Development projects.
U.S.S.R.	Equipment	2 hospitals, secondary school, radio
	$44 million credits	station, government printing plant.

[1]The countries were chosen as being illustrative of the important role played by bilateral aid in African foreign relations. The recipient states attempt to maintain a balance among the donors in order to preserve their posture of non-alignment in world affairs.

Source: Honorable Allen J. Ellender, *A Report on United States Foreign Operations in Africa.* Senate Document No. 8, 88th Congress, 1st session. U.S. Government Printing Office, Washington: 1963.

IV. The Search for African Unity

FRENCH AFRICAN FEDERATIONS

From 1904 to 1958 France's colonies in continental Africa were grouped into two federations: French West Africa (AOF), with its capital at Dakar, and French Equatorial Africa (AEF), with its capital at Brazzaville. The first step in the disintegration of these federations was the passage in 1956 of the *loi cadre* (outline law) which granted autonomy to the individual territories and greatly increased their power in relation to that of the federations. This process of decentralization culminated in 1958 with the construction of the French Community of autonomous states. Although the Community did not explicitly grant independence to its African members, the latter considered that independence was implicit in Community membership. By 1960 all former members of AEF and AOF had sought and gained that independence.

Although the former members of AOF have not maintained any formal ties, the former members of AEF cooperate in matters of defense, commerce, transportation, communication, and geological research.

The Search For African Unity — Past and Present

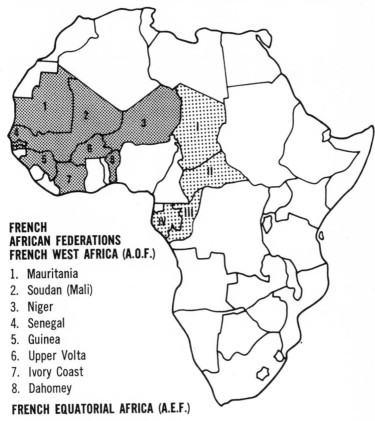

**FRENCH
AFRICAN FEDERATIONS
FRENCH WEST AFRICA (A.O.F.)**

1. Mauritania
2. Soudan (Mali)
3. Niger
4. Senegal
5. Guinea
6. Upper Volta
7. Ivory Coast
8. Dahomey

FRENCH EQUATORIAL AFRICA (A.E.F.)

I. Chad
II. Ubangi-Shari (Central African Republic)
III. Middle Congo (Republic of Congo (Brazzaville)
IV. Gabon

INTER-AFRICAN AND MALAGASY STATES ORGANIZATION (Monrovia Group)

The Monrovia Conference of May 1961 was the largest convocation of representatives of African states up until that time. At this conference the delegates of twenty countries adopted a set of broad principles governing their relations among their states and outlining procedures to assist in the pacific settlement of disputes arising among them. A second conference was held in January 1962, in Lagos, Nigeria, to which were invited the leaders of all independent African states (except South Africa). Although eight of those invited did not attend (due to the absence of the Algerian Provisional Government), the Lagos Conference achieved marked success in institutionalizing African cooperation. The Charter which was proposed and later ratified called for the establishment of a permanent secretariat, an assembly of heads of states and government, a council of ministers, and organs for coordinating economic policy and mediating disputes. The appeal of the Monrovia Group for "not ... political integration ... but unity of aspirations and of action," and the offer of membership to any independent African state "under indigenous African rule" helped pave the way for the wider unity achieved at Addis Ababa in May 1963.

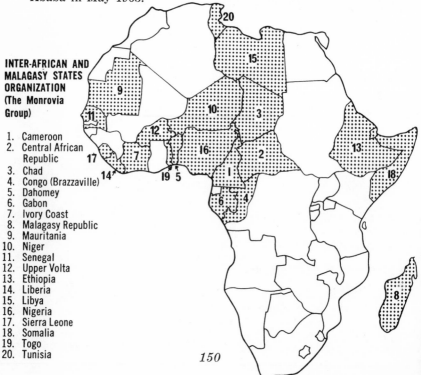

INTER-AFRICAN AND MALAGASY STATES ORGANIZATION (The Monrovia Group)

1. Cameroon
2. Central African Republic
3. Chad
4. Congo (Brazzaville)
5. Dahomey
6. Gabon
7. Ivory Coast
8. Malagasy Republic
9. Mauritania
10. Niger
11. Senegal
12. Upper Volta
13. Ethiopia
14. Liberia
15. Libya
16. Nigeria
17. Sierra Leone
18. Somalia
19. Togo
20. Tunisia

EAST AFRICAN
COMMON SERVICES ORGANIZATION

This coordinating body is one of the most successful functional organizations in Africa. Established in 1962 to carry on the operations of the former East Africa High Commission, it has policy-making power over the administration of communications, finance, commerce, industry, and social and research services. The railway, harbor, postal, tax and other systems all are operated in common. It was expected that this close technical cooperation would lay the groundwork for the creation of a political federation, embracing Tanganyika, Kenya, Uganda, and Zanzibar. Although such a federation would be in keeping with the provision of the Charter of the Organization of African Unity for regional groupings, various disputes and uncertainties have impeded efforts to achieve unity.

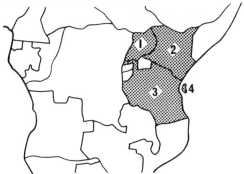

**EAST AFRICAN
COMMON SERVICES
ORGANIZATION (E.A.C.S.O.)**

1. Uganda
2. Kenya
3. Tanganyika
4. Zanzibar
   (Associate
   member)

ORGANIZATION OF AFRICAN UNITY

The culminating step toward African unity was the signing of the Charter of the Organization of African Unity by thirty states in Addis Ababa on May 25, 1963. The purpose of the OAU is "to promote the unity and solidarity of the African states." Members agreed to coordinate their diplomacy; economic development and planning; educational and cultural programs; health, sanitation, and nutrition; scientific and technical advances; defense and security. The formal institutions of the OAU include the Assembly of Heads of State and Government, and the Council of Ministers. The Assembly has the power to establish specialized commissions and the Council's task is to implement the decisions of the Assembly. The OAU is administered by a General Secretariat, of international civil servants. A Commission of Mediation is charged with settling disputes arising among member states.

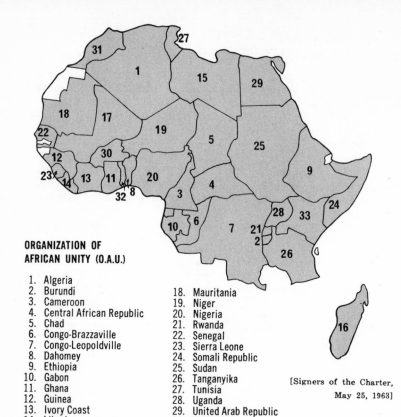

ORGANIZATION OF AFRICAN UNITY (O.A.U.)

1. Algeria
2. Burundi
3. Cameroon
4. Central African Republic
5. Chad
6. Congo-Brazzaville
7. Congo-Leopoldville
8. Dahomey
9. Ethiopia
10. Gabon
11. Ghana
12. Guinea
13. Ivory Coast
14. Liberia
15. Libya
16. Malagasy Republic
17. Mali

18. Mauritania
19. Niger
20. Nigeria
21. Rwanda
22. Senegal
23. Sierra Leone
24. Somali Republic
25. Sudan
26. Tanganyika
27. Tunisia
28. Uganda
29. United Arab Republic
30. Upper Volta
31. Morocco*
32. Togo*
33. Kenya**

[Signers of the Charter,
May 25, 1963]

*adhered later
**pledged to adhere

COUNCIL OF THE ENTENTE

1. Dahomey
2. Ivory Coast
3. Niger
4. Upper Volta

COUNCIL OF THE ENTENTE

This body, formed in 1959, brings together the heads of state, presidents, and vice presidents of the legislative assemblies, and certain ministers of Dahomey, Ivory Coast, Niger, and Upper Volta in biannual sessions to discuss matters of common interest. It is a loosely structured group which seeks to coordinate fiscal and commercial policies and public services. One of the central institutions is a Solidarity Fund for mutual economic assistance. The members of the Entente, considering their functional group consistent with the principles of the Charter of the Organization of African Unity signed in May 1963, have resisted pressure from other African states to disband.

PAN-AFRICAN FREEDOM MOVEMENT OF EAST, CENTRAL AND SOUTHERN AFRICA

Founded in 1958, PAFMECSA was dedicated to the achievement and consolidation of the independence of all of Africa. With headquarters in Dar-es-Salaam, Tanganyika, it served to link the liberation movements of the remaining colonial dependencies with the independent states of Africa. In September 1963, however, PAFMECSA'S leaders announced its forthcoming dissolution, its functions to be taken over by the nine member Coordinating Committee of the Organization of African Unity.

(PAFMECSA)

1. Uganda
2. Kenya
3. Rwanda
4. Burundi
5. Republic of the Congo (Leopoldville)
6. Tanganyika
7. Zanzibar
8. Northern Rhodesia (Zambia)
9. Nyasaland (Malawi)
10. Southern Rhodesia (Zimbabwe)
11. Mozambique
12. South Africa
13. Angola
14. Mauritius
15. Ethiopia
16. Somalia
17. South West Africa
18. Basutoland
19. Bechuanaland
20. Swaziland

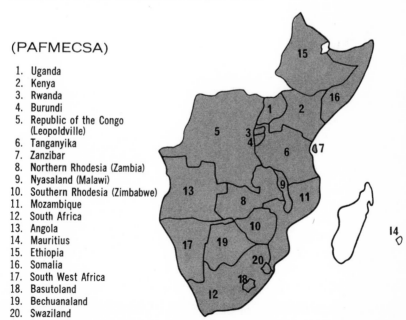

CASABLANCA GROUP

The meeting which led to the formation of the Brazzaville Group was quickly followed by a second gathering of a group of powers at Casablanca, Morocco, on January 7, 1961. The Casablanca Group supported the position of Patrice Lumumba in the post-independence struggle for power in the Congo, the claim of Morocco for suzerainty over Mauretania, and the anti-Israeli policies of the United Arab Republic. Four permanent committees were established to coordinate policy in the fields of politics, economics, culture, and defense. Although the Charter called for establishment of an African Consultative Assembly and several other organs, only an African Telecommunications Union actually materialized. The Casablanca Group was formally dissolved after the founding of the Organization of African Unity in 1963.

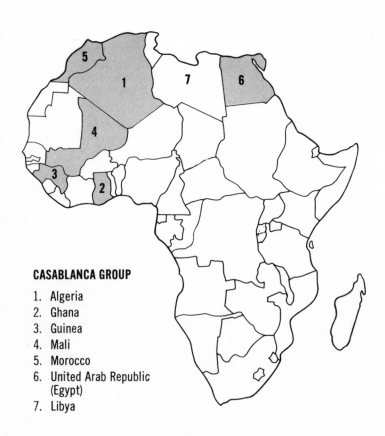

CASABLANCA GROUP

1. Algeria
2. Ghana
3. Guinea
4. Mali
5. Morocco
6. United Arab Republic (Egypt)
7. Libya

UNION OF AFRICAN STATES AND MADAGASCAR (U.A.M.) (Brazzaville Group)

The desire of the former French African territories to mediate between France and Algeria led to the convoking of this group in Brazzaville in December 1960. Out of this and subsequent meetings developed common organizations for defense, economic cooperation, communication, air transportation, banking, and scientific research. With the formation of the Inter-African and Malagasy Organization, the U.A.M. became a sub-group within a larger framework. The U.A.M. recently has come under attack from non-members as being contrary to the Charter of African Unity, even though the latter allows for "regional" groupings. Its members have resolved to maintain its existence until such time as a gradual merger with the Organization of African Unity can be effected which would not be detrimental to their position. As a first step they agreed to dissolve the U.A.M. group at the United Nations.

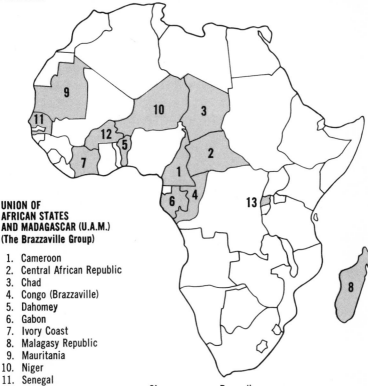

UNION OF AFRICAN STATES AND MADAGASCAR (U.A.M.) (The Brazzaville Group)

1. Cameroon
2. Central African Republic
3. Chad
4. Congo (Brazzaville)
5. Dahomey
6. Gabon
7. Ivory Coast
8. Malagasy Republic
9. Mauritania
10. Niger
11. Senegal
12. Upper Volta
13. Rwanda

Observers: a. Burundi
b. Republic of the Congo (Leopoldville)

BIBLIOGRAPHY

Apter, David E. *Ghana in Transition*. New York: Atheneum, 1963.

―――. *The Political Kingdom in Uganda*. Princeton: Princeton University Press, 1961.

Awolowo, Obafemi. *AWO*. Cambridge: Cambridge University Press, 1960.

Azikiwe, Nnamdi. *ZIK*. Cambridge: Cambridge University Press, 1961.

Bascom, William R., and Melville J. Herskovitz (eds.). *Continuity and Change in African Cultures*. Chicago: University of Chicago Press, 1959.

Baulin, Jacques. *The Arab Role in Africa*. Baltimore: Penguin Books, 1962.

Bello, Alhaji Sir Ahmadu. *My Life*. Cambridge: Cambridge University Press, 1962.

Boyd, Andrew, and Patrick van Rensburg. *An Atlas of African Affairs*. New York: Praeger, 1962.

Carter, Gwendolen M. *The Politics of Inequality: South Africa Since 1948*. New York: Praeger, 1958.

―――― (ed.). *African One-Party States*. Ithaca: Cornell University Press, 1962.

―――― (ed.). *Five African States: Responses to Diversity*. Ithaca: Cornell University Press, 1963.

Cohen, Andrew. *British Policy in Changing Africa*. Evanston: Northwestern University Press, 1959.

Coleman, James S. *Nigeria: Background to Nationalism*. Berkeley: University of California Press, 1958.

―――. "The Politics of Sub-Saharan Africa." In Gabriel A. Almond and James S. Coleman (eds.), *The Politics of the Developing Areas*. Princeton: Princeton University Press, 1960.

———— and Belmont Brice, Jr. "The Role of the Military in Sub-Saharan Africa." In John J. Johnson (ed.), *The Role of the Military in Underdeveloped Countries*. Princeton: Princeton University Press, 1962.

Cowan, L. Gray. *Local Government in West Africa*. New York: Columbia University Press, 1958.

Crowder, Michael. *Senegal*. London: Oxford University Press, 1962. (For the Institute of Race Relations.)

Davidson, Basil. *Old Africa Rediscovered*. Garden City: Doubleday, 1960.

Duffy, James. *Portugal in Africa*. Baltimore: Penguin Books, 1963.

Emerson, Rupert. *From Empire to Nation*. Boston: Beacon Press, 1960.

Evans-Pritchard, E. C., and M. M. Fortes (eds.). *African Political Systems*. London: Oxford University Press, 1940; reprinted 1961. (For the International African Institute.)

Fage, J. D. *An Atlas of African History*. London: Edward Arnold, Ltd., 1959.

————. *An Introduction to the History of West Africa*. Cambridge: Cambridge University Press, 1955.

Franck, Thomas M. *Race and Nationalism: The Struggle for Power in Rhodesia-Nyasaland*. New York: Fordham University Press, 1960.

Hailey, Lord Malcolm. *An African Survey*. Rev. ed. London: Oxford University Press, 1957.

Hance, William. *African Economic Development*. New York: Harper, 1958. (For the Council on Foreign Relations.)

Hodgkin, Thomas L. *African Political Parties*. Harmondsworth: Penguin Books, 1961.

————. *Nationalism in Colonial Africa*. London: Muller, 1956.

———— and Ruth Schachter. *French-Speaking West Africa in Transition*. (International Conciliation no. 528.) New York: Carnegie Endowment for International Peace, 1960.

Horrabin, J. F. *An Atlas of Africa*. New York: Praeger, 1961.

Hovet, Thomas, Jr. *Africa in the United Nations.* Evanston: Northwestern University Press, 1963.

Hunter, Guy. *The New Societies of Tropical Africa.* London: Oxford University Press, 1962. (For the Institute of Race Relations.)

Ingham, Kenneth. *A History of East Africa.* New York: Praeger, 1963.

Kaunda, Kenneth. *Zambia Shall Be Free.* New York: Praeger, 1963.

Kenyatta, Jomo. *Facing Mount Kenya.* London: Secker and Warburg, 1938; reprinted 1953.

Kimble, George H. T. *Tropical Africa.* 2 vols. New York: The Twentieth Century Fund, 1960.

Legum, Colin. *Pan-Africanism.* New York: Praeager, 1962.

———— (ed.). *Africa: A Handbook to the Continent.* New York: Praeger, 1962.

Luthuli, Albert. *Let My People Go.* New York: McGraw-Hill, 1962.

Lystad, Robert A. *The Ashanti — A Proud People.* New Brunswick: Rutgers University Press, 1958.

Máir, Lucy. *Primitive Government.* Baltimore: Penguin Books, 1962.

Mboya, Tom. *Freedom and After.* Boston: Little, Brown and Co., 1963.

Merriam, Alan P. *Congo: Background and Conflict.* Evanston: Northwestern University Press, 1961.

Murdock, George Peter. *Africa: Its Peoples and Their Culture History.* New York: McGraw-Hill, 1959.

Nkrumah, Kwame. *Africa Must Unite.* New York: Praeger, 1963.

————. *Autobiography.* New York: Thomas Nelson, 1957.

————. *I Speak of Freedom.* New York: Praeger, 1961.

Padmore, George. *Pan Africanism or Communism?* New York: Roy Publishers, 1956.

Sigmund, Paul E., Jr. *The Ideologies of the Developing Nations.* New York: Praeger, 1963.

Sklar, Richard. *Political Parties in Nigeria.* Princeton: Princeton University Press, 1963.

Thompson, Virginia, and Richard Adloff. *The Emerging States of French Equatorial Africa.* London: Oxford University Press, 1960.

————. *French West Africa.* Palo Alto: Stanford University Press, 1957.

Tilman, Robert O., and Taylor Cole (eds.). *The Nigerian Political Scene.* Durham: Duke University Press. (For the Commonwealth Studies Center.)

Touré, Sekou. *African Independence and Unity.* New York: Colby Printers, 1959.

Turnbull, Colin M. *The Lonely African.* 2nd ed. New York: Doubleday & Company (Anchor Books), 1963.

Wallerstein, Immanuel. *Africa: The Politics of Independence.* New York: Random House (Vintage Books), 1961.

Zolberg, Aristide. *One-Party Government in the Ivory Coast.* Princeton: Princeton University Press, 1964.

Index

Gabon, 71
Ghana, 13, 27, 31, 37, 60
Ghana-Guinea union, 60
Government, economic control, 32
  European control, 44
  and industrialization, 32-35
Great Britain, 39, 47-48, 49, 51, 78
Grey, Robert F., 11n., 12
Guinea, 5, 31, 35, 37, 39, 41

Houphouet-Boigny, Felix, 59, 71

Ideology, Africa and East-West
  conflict, 21
  party and leader, 18
Imperialism, 20
Independence, political
  pattern, 6-7
Individualism, 22-23
Industrialization, 24-25, 33
  and capital, 33
  and political stability, 34-35
  and technical skill, 33-34
Inter-African and Malagasy
  States Organization, 64
Interest groups, 23-28
International Development
  Association, 40
International Finance
  Corporation, 40

Kariba Dam, 40
Katanga, 37, 77
Kaunda, Kenneth, 50
Keita, Madeira, 8
Kenya, 4, 7, 42-44, 54
Kenyatta, Jomo, 3, 54, 60

Labor unions, 24
  See also Trade union movement
Lagos Charter, 64
Leader, and economic
  dependence, 38-39
  and military group, 26
  and modernization, 14
  and one-party system, 16-18
Leadership, and economic
  independence, 30
  methods of change, 17
  nationalist parties, 2-3
  of Pan-Africanism, 68-70
  and party ideology, 5
  and youth movement, 27
Liberia, 37
Lumumba, Patrice, 77

Malawi, 46-51
Malawi Congress Party, 50
Mali, 8, 39, 60
Marxist-Leninist ideology, 2,
  18, 20, 22
Mau Mau, 54
Mauritania, 61
Military coup, 26
Military establishment, 25-26
Mineral resources, 37-38
Modernization, and instability,
  13-14
Monrovia group, 64, 77, 79
Morocco, V, 61
Mozambique, 42, 51-53

Nasser, Gamal Abdel, 61
National liberation, and
  unification, 77
National unity, and independence,
  5-6
Nationalism, 1-6, 42
Nationalist parties, 2-5
  and industrialization, 34
Nationalist Party (South
  Africa), 46
Nationalist Party (Southern
  Rhodesia), 50
Nationalization, 35
Négritude, 57
Neutralism, 21, 78-79
Nigeria, 5, 6, 7, 13, 26, 27, 32, 78
Nkomo, Joshua, 50
Nkrumah, Kwame, 3, 14, 18, 19,
  33, 56, 57, 59, 68, 80
Nkrumahism, 18, 21
Nyerere, Julius, 9-10, 16

OAMCE, *see* Organisation Afro-
  Malagache de Coopération
  Economique
OAU, *see* Organization of
  African Unity
One-party system, 7-15
  and constitutional procedures,
  17
  evolution to multi-party, 28-29
  and industrialization, 34
  and interest groups, 28-29
  See also Leader
Opposition, to nationalism, 4
  party, 9
  repression, 9
Organisation Afro-Malagache de
  Coopération Economique

161

(OAMCE), 63
Organization of African Unity,
  59, 66-68

Padmore, George, 59, 60
PAFMECSA, *see* Pan-African
  Freedom Movement
  of East Central and Southern
  Africa (PAFMECSA), 65,
  72, 73
Pan Africanism, 59-60, 68-70,
  74-76
  barriers to unity, 69-70
Pan-Africanist Conference
  (Manchester, 1945), 60
Parliament, and one-party system,
  10-11
Parliamentary procedure, 12
Parti de la Fédération Africaine,
  IX
Parti Démocratique de Guinée,
  18, 19, 22, 35, 75
PDG, *see* Parti Démocratique
  de Guinée
Population, 42
Portugal, 42, 51-53
Power, personalized, 16-17
Preventive Detention Act, 15
Pye, Lucian, 14

Raw material economy, 30-31
Religious interest groups, 27
  and nationalism, 2
Republic of South Africa, 42,
  44, 45-46
Roberto, Holden, 53
Ruanda, 65
Rural area, development, 37
  and nationalism, 2

Senegal, IX, 26, 27
Senghor, Léopold, IX, 19, 26, 57
Sigmund, Paul, *The Ideologies
  of the Developing Nations,*
  9n.
Socialism, 18-23
  "African," 18, 19-20, 21, 76
South Africa, *see* Republic of
  South Africa
Southern Rhodesia, 45, 46-51
Soviet Union, economic aid, 40
Standard of living, 38
State, multi-racial, 43, 46

non-racial, 43
Sudan, 26

Tanganyika, 9
Thiam, Doudou, 57
Togo, 13, 26
Touré, Sekou, 5, 18, 19, 22
Trade, intra-African, 31, 39, 58,
  71-72
Trade union movement, 2
Tribe, and national unity, 5
  and nationalism, 4
  political system, 11-12
Tshombe, Moise, 77

UAM, *see* Union of African
  States and Madagascar
Unification, administrative, 58
  differences, 65
  economic, 58, 63
  federal structure, 56
  future, 68-76
  gradual, 59, 62-65
  immediate, 59-61
  and non-Africans, 76
  regional, 65, 72-73
Union of African States and
  Madagascar (UAM), 63-64
Union Afro-Malagache de
  Coopération Économique, 73
Union Sudanaise, 8
UNIP, *see* United National
  Independence Party
United Federal Party, 49
United National Independence
  Party (UNIP), 50
United Nations, 40, 80
United States, aid, 40-41
United States of Africa, 60
Upper Volta, 62
Urban area, development, 37
  groups, 24
  nationalism, 1

Violence, and independence, 4

Welensky, Sir Roy, 49, 50
West, political institutions
  in Africa, 10-11
World Bank, 40

Youth groups, 26-27

Zambia, 37, 45, 46-51